TOP **10**
TORONTO

LORRAINE JOHNSON &
BARBARA HOPKINSON

D0360300

EYEWITNESS TRAVEL

Contents

Left **View from the Toronto Islands** Right **Victorian houses, Cabbagetown**

LONDON, NEW YORK,
MELBOURNE, MUNICH AND DELHI
www.dk.com

Produced by
International Book Productions Inc., Toronto

Reproduced by Colourscan, Singapore
Printed and bound in China by South China
Printing Co. Ltd.

First American Edition, 2005
09 10 9 8 7 6 5 4 3 2 1

Published in the United States by
DK Publishing, Inc.,
375 Hudson Street, New York,
New York 10014

A cataloging in publication record is available
from the Library of Congress

ISSN 1479-344X
ISBN 978-0-75664-237-2

Within each Top 10 list in this book, no hierarchy
of quality or popularity is implied. All 10 are, in
the editor's opinion, of roughly equal merit.

We're trying to be cleaner and greener:

- we recycle waste and switch things off
- we use paper from responsibly managed forests whenever possible
- we ask our printers to actively reduce water and energy consumption
- we check out our suppliers' working conditions – they never use child labour

Find out more about our values and
best practices at www.dk.com

Contents

Toronto's Top 10

The information in this DK Eyewitness Top 10 Travel Guide is checked regularly.
Every effort has been made to ensure that this book is as up-to-date as possible at the time
of going to press. Some details, however, such as telephone numbers, opening hours, prices,
gallery hanging arrangements and travel information are liable to change. The publishers
cannot accept responsibility for any consequences arising from the use of this book, nor for
any material on third party websites, and cannot guarantee that any website address in this
book will be a suitable source of travel information. We value the views and suggestions of
our readers very highly. Please write to: Publisher, DK Eyewitness Travel Guides,
Dorling Kindersley, 80 Strand, London, WC2R 0RL Great Britain.

COVER: Front – **DK IMAGES:** Cylla Von Tiedemann bl; **GETTY IMAGES:** Chris Thomaidis main.
Spine: **DK IMAGES** Francesca Yorke b. Back: **Zefa Visual Media:** Masterfile/Brian Sytnyk tr;
DK IMAGES: Peter Wilson tc; Francesca Yorke tl;

Left **Cinesphere, Ontario Place** Right **Lifeguard station, Ashbridges Bay**

Contents

Left **Galleria, BCE Place** Right **Princes' Gate, Canadian National Exhibition**

TORONTO'S
TOP 10

TORONTO'S TOP 10

TOP10 Toronto Highlights

Torontonians are justifiably proud of their vibrant and exciting metropolis. Canada's largest city and its financial hub, Toronto has a tremendous amount to offer, including a thriving theater, music, and arts scene, top museums, world-class restaurants and shops, a beautiful lakeside location with lovely beaches, and streets safe and inviting to walk in. Its cultural diversity – over 90 ethnic groups are represented in Toronto – enhances the urban experience.

Royal Ontario Museum 1
A treasure-trove of ancient mummies, exquisitely decorated period rooms, huge dinosaurs, stuffed birds, stunning Chinese art, and imposing Greek and Roman sculptures are among the many rewarding sights to be seen during a visit to this wonderful museum *(see pp8–11)*.

CN Tower & Its Views 2
High-speed elevators mounted on the outside of this, the world's tallest telecommunications tower, whisk you up 181 stories to an unforgettable view of the city *(see pp12–13)*.

Toronto Islands 3
A short ferry ride from downtown, this chain of small islands provides a respite from summer heat with its beaches, picnic grounds, and amusement park *(see pp14–15)*.

Art Gallery of Ontario 4
A fabulous museum, with excellent collections of Canadian art, including that of contemporary artist Michael Snow *(below)*, Inuit art, French Impressionists, photography, prints and drawings, and a 19th-century house, The Grange *(see pp16–17)*.

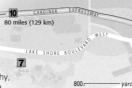

Casa Loma 5
Built by financier Sir Henry Pellatt, this turreted mansion, with its 98 grand rooms and beautiful gardens, provides a glimpse of turn-of-the-19th-century luxury *(see pp18–19)*.

Distillery Historic District

Once the largest distillery in North America, this former industrial complex is one of Toronto's hottest destinations. Victorian buildings and cobblestoned streets provide an unforgettable backdrop to the many unusual stores and galleries, and excellent restaurants and cafés found here (see pp20–21).

Ontario Place

Its lakeside location makes this fun-filled playground a popular place to spend a summer day with the family. Children delight in the many water rides; an IMAX theater and concert amphitheater appeal to all ages (see pp22–3).

Eaton Centre

Toronto's pre-eminent downtown mall, named after a now-defunct department-store chain, is conveniently located near several major hotels and attractions. If you are looking for a one-stop shopping destination, this mall, selling everything from batteries to hockey sticks, is it (see pp24–5).

Hockey Hall of Fame

Irrespective of their age, most visitors to Toronto who are ice hockey fans make a pilgrimage here to see such revered relics as the original Stanley Cup, shoot pucks at a video goalie, walk through the re-creation of a locker room, and watch some of hockey's sterling moments in the Broadcast Zone (see pp26–7).

Map labels: RENPORT ROAD, AVENUE ROAD, YONGE STREET, Yorkville, BLOOR ST EAST, Queen's Park, BAY STREET, YONGE STREET, JARVIS STREET, CARLTON ST, UNIVERSITY AVENUE, BAY STREET, DUNDAS ST EAST, QUEEN ST WEST, QUEEN ST EAST, Downtown, KING ST WEST, KING ST EAST, BAY STREET, YONGE STREET, JARVIS STREET, GARDINER EXPRESSWAY, QUEENS QUAY EAST, Toronto Inner Harbour, 1 mile (1.6 km)

Niagara Falls

After the two-hour drive from Toronto, stand on Table Rock for a look at one of the world's wonders, the magnificent Horseshoe Falls, where the Niagara River plunges 176 ft (53 m) over a 1060-ft- (323-m-) long precipice. The town of Niagara Falls and outlying area offer fine dining, entertainment, winery tours, historic museums, and more (see pp28–31).

Toronto's Top 10

📑10 Royal Ontario Museum

Canada's largest museum, with more than five million objects, the Royal Ontario Museum, or ROM, was created in 1912 with the ambitious dual mandate of showcasing human civilization and the natural world. Galleries of archeology, science, art, and nature display significant collections of Chinese treasures, ornate mummy cases, and perennially popular dinosaur skeletons. Hands-on exhibits invite children to excavate for fossils and examine species under a microscope.

Museum façade

🍴 Grab a quick bite in the cafeteria on the lower level, or settle in for a fine meal at the rooftop restaurant, C5.

⏰ Fall to spring, visit on Friday evenings to catch film screenings and free concerts, along with half-price admission.

Replicas of various items in the collections are on offer at the gift shops.

• 100 Queen's Park Cres; however, the main entrance is around the corner on Bloor St W, just west of Queen's Park
• Map C3
• 416 586 8000
• www.rom.on.ca
• Open 10am–5:30pm daily (until 9:30pm Fri)
• Adm rates vary per exhibition

Top 10 Features
1. Djedmaatesankh Mummy
2. *Allosaurus* Dinosaurs
3. Acropolis Model
4. Living Beehive
5. Mosaic Dome
6. English Parlor
7. Ming Tomb
8. Crest Poles
9. Chinese Guardian Lions
10. Hardwood Forest

1 Djedmaatesankh Mummy
Richly decorated with gold leaf and hieroglyphic inscriptions, this ancient Egyptian sarcophagus *(below)*, which dates back to around 850 BC, protects the mummified body of a court musician. Although museum researchers have never opened the case, a high-tech CAT scan has revealed that she died at age 35 from a severe tooth abscess.

2 *Allosaurus* Dinosaurs
With heads rearing and jaws open, these two menacing Jurassic carnivores lunge after their prey, a bony-plated *Stegosaurus*. The skeletons *(above)* are lightweight casts of the original bones.

3 Acropolis Model
The Golden Age of Athens – about 400 BC – comes alive in this model of Greek temple life, which depicts the Parthenon and surrounding buildings as they looked at the height of ancient Greek civilization.

4 Living Beehive
This active beehive is a highlight of the Hands-On Biodiversity Gallery. Visitors can see the interior of the hive, buzzing with thousands of honey bees that have flown in from the outdoors.

Mosaic Dome
A spectacular mosaic dome tops the rotunda. Over a million tiny colored squares of Venetian glass form symbols of ancient cultures, such as an Inca thunder god and a mythical Greek seahorse.

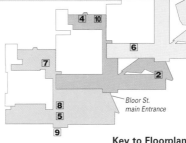

English Parlor
Dating from the 1750s, with original carved pine walls and period furniture, this parlor *(right)* looks as if a wealthy English gentleman and his card-playing friends have only momentarily left the room. Though the gilded harp in the corner is silent, evocative, ambient Baroque music completes the vignette.

Ming Tomb
Guarded by stone camels, a fierce warrior, and a scepter-bearing adviser, this ensemble of funerary sculpture features artifacts from the Yuan dynasty (14th century), Ming dynasty (15th–17th centuries), and Qing dynasty (17th–18th centuries). Sculpted mythological animals adorn the arches.

Crest Poles
Four striking crest poles, the stylized figures commemorating family origins and achievements, were carved out of western red cedar in the 1880s by the Nisga'a and Haida peoples of Canada's northwest coast. The tallest is over 80 ft (24 m) high.

Chinese Guardian Lions
Two proud stone lions, carved for a Beijing palace in the 1600s, stand guard outside the museum.

Hardwood Forest
The dappled light and hushed calm of an Ontario hardwood forest are perfectly re-created in this diorama *(below)*. If you look closely, you will see more than 20 animals, among them a porcupine and fox, hiding among the colorful autumn leaves.

Bloor St. main Entrance

Key to Floorplan
▢	Level 1
▢	Level 2
▢	Level 3

Museum Guide
The ROM has undergone a massive expansion, adding 56,000 sq ft (5200 sq m) of exhibition space within a unique crystal structure. Level 1 includes the Korea, China, and Japan collections, and two galleries exploring the development of Canada as a nation – First Peoples and Canadian Heritage. Natural history is the focus of Level 2, with galleries on minerals and gems, evolution, and dinosaurs. Level 3 features anthropology and archeology, with artifacts from Africa, the Americas, Asia Pacific, Egypt, and Rome, as well as 20th-century art and design. Textiles and the Institute for Contemporary Culture are on Level 4.

In the CIBC Discovery Room (Level 2) young visitors can try on armour, examine specimens, and dig for dinosaur bones

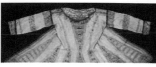 

Left **Inuit coat, First Peoples Gallery** Right **Ming Dynasty headrest, Chinese Art Collection**

TOP 10 Collections

1 Dinosaurs
The popular Dinosaur Gallery, located in the Michael A. Lee-Chin Crystal, is home to almost 20 full dinosaur skeletons, of both marine and land dwellers, including the world's most complete *Maiasaura* and her baby, which are thought to be 80 million years old.

2 Hands-On Biodiversity
Children and adults alike are encouraged to get up close and personal with the wonders of the natural world in this imaginative discovery zone on Third Level. Touch animal skulls, antlers, and pelts, and don special glasses to look at the world through the "eyes" of various animals.

3 Canada's First Peoples
The ROM's holdings of Aboriginal artifacts, on Street Level, are superb. National treasures include an Innu-painted caribou-skin coat and a quilled pouch collected by Canadian painter Paul Kane (1810–71), who traveled extensively among Native settlements in the mid-1800s. You won't be able to miss the Umyak boat, large enough to hold an entire Indian village.

4 Ancient Egypt
More than 1,000 artifacts, from everyday gold earrings to elaborate ceremonial mummy cases, combine to shed light on ancient Egypt (Third Level). The Punt Wall, a plaster cast taken from the temple of Queen Hatsheput near present-day Somalia, provides an opportunity to test your skill at decoding hieroglyphics.

5 Ice-Age Mammals
The rise of mammals following the Ice Age's "big chill," which ended about 10,000 years ago, is explored in this dramatic exhibit on Third Level. A giant beaver, mastodon, saber-toothed cat, and hippopotamus are just some of the impressive specimens on display.

6 Birds
Hundreds of birds from all over the world swoop together in one spectacular flock, suspended in mid-flight from the ceiling of the Michael A. Lee-Chin Crystal. Marvel at the 9-ft (2.7-m) wing span of the albatross *(left)*; listen to birdsongs at interactive booths; and pull out drawers containing nests, bones, eggs, and feathers.

7 Art Deco
Rare French and American Art Deco furniture, lamps, and sculpture – exquisitely crafted from ebony, lacquer, and ivory, among other fine materials – celebrate this influential design movement of the 1920s and 1930s. Art Deco glass, ceramic, and silver pieces round out this collection, on Third Level.

Top 10 Architectural Highlights

1. Rotunda
2. Crest Poles
3. Queen's Park façade
4. Stained-glass windows, Queen's Park entrance
5. ROM Theatre
6. Glass Room
7. Floor mosaic at entrance to Samuel European Galleries
8. Leaded windows in stairwells
9. Arched windows along western façade
10. Exterior cornice around building

The Crystal

The highlight of the museum's renovation is the Michael A. Lee-Chin Crystal, a magnificent glass and aluminum-clad addition designed by world-renowned architect Daniel Libeskind and named for the lead donor. This jagged crystalline structure of interlocking forms, with its spectacular atrium space, glass-sliver windows, and jutting angles thrusting over the sidewalk, is the dramatic new entrance to the museum. Inside the Crystal, which has been designed to have no right angles, are four levels of galleries, including two unusual spaces: the Spirit House, a soaring void criss-crossed by bridges linking the new galleries, and the Stair of Wonders, an intriguing vertical cabinet of curiosities from the ROM's collection. The Crystal is linked on all levels except the fourth to the original building.

The Michael A. Lee-Chin Crystal, with the historic building to the left

Chinese Art

8 Spanning over 6,000 years of Chinese history (4500 BC to AD 1900), this collection (Street Level) ranks among the world's finest. The procession of 7th-century ceramic tomb figures and the monumental Buddhist sculptures from the 12th to 16th centuries are outstanding.

Arms and Armor

9 On Third Level, intimidating battle gear stands guard over some 300 pieces – from 15th-century European chain mail to World War I automatic weapons – that highlight the history of human conflict.

Greek Sculpture

10 Striking stone, bronze, and ivory sculptures make this collection on Third Level one of the best in North America. Those dating back to the Hellenistic Age, around 325 BC, reflect the development of Greek society under Alexander the Great as his army forged into Egypt and India.

ᵀᴼᴾ10 CN Tower & Its Views

A 58-second elevator ride whisks you to the 114th story of the world's tallest free-standing structure, the 181-story, 1,815.5-ft (553.5-m) communications tower built by Canadian National Railway in 1976. Breathtaking views from the glass-fronted elevator set the stage for even more dizzying sights from the Look Out, where on a clear day you can see as far as the Canada-US border. Visitors with nerves of steel can walk on the Glass Floor for a view 1,122 ft (342 m) straight down. For panoramic views 1,465 ft (447 m) above the ground, take an elevator up 33 more stories to Sky Pod, the world's highest man-made observatory.

The Glass Floor

🍽 Stop in at Horizons Café on the Look Out level for casual fare and spectacular views. Or reserve a table at the revolving 360 restaurant (416 362 5411) to enjoy fine dining and a view that changes slowly throughout the meal.

🛍 Shop for one-of-a-kind souvenirs and authentic Canadiana at the Marketplace.

Test your skills with the multimedia motion-simulation games at Edge Arcade or catch a short film on the tower's construction at the Maple Leaf Cinema.

• 301 Front St W
• Map J5
• 416 868 6937
• www.cntower.ca
• Open 9am–10pm Sun–Thu, 9am–10:30pm Fri–Sat; closed Dec 25
• Adm prices vary between attractions

Top 10 Views

1. Toronto Islands
2. Eaton Centre
3. Toronto Music Garden
4. Financial District
5. Urban Forest
6. Roy Thomson Hall
7. Union Station
8. City Hall
9. Fort York
10. Niagara Falls

1 Toronto Islands
A ribbon of islands *(above) (see pp14–15)* shelters Toronto's harbor and provides a car-free retreat just a short ferry ride from downtown. The islands have bike paths, picnic areas, beaches and boardwalk, and an amusement park *(see p49).*

2 Eaton Centre
Tourists and locals alike flock here for the hundreds of shops and eateries *(see pp24–5).* The glass vaulted roof is modeled on Milan's 19th-century Galleria Vittorio Emanuele.

3 Toronto Music Garden
The garden's design, inspired by the music of Baroque composer J. S. Bach, is best seen from above; the swirling pathways and plantings do indeed seem musical *(below).*

➡ *At the heart of City Hall's plaza is the Peace Garden. The roof of the structure within is "damaged," to symbolize world conflict*

Financial District
Soaring towers, such as those of the modernist Toronto-Dominion Centre *(see p64)*, signal the heart of Toronto's – and Canada's – financial district *(right)*. The nation's major banks, insurance companies, and stockbrokers ply their trades as wind-jostled workers hurry along canyon-like streets.

Urban Forest
One look at Toronto from above and it's clear it's a green city: stately canopy trees line streets and snake along ravines.

Roy Thomson Hall
The space-age design of this music hall, in the core of the theater district, features a distinctive glass canopy *(see p44)*.

Union Station
A relic from the days when passenger rail was Canada's primary mode of transportation, this station *(above)* has lost none of its grandeur since it opened in 1927, still serving as an impressive gateway to the city *(see p66)*.

Fort York
Founded in 1793 and the site of the 1813 Battle of York, in which the fort was destroyed and then rebuilt, Fort York *(right)* has Canada's best collection of buildings from the War of 1812 era. Eight original structures stand on this triangular piece of land, among them blockhouses, barracks, and officers' quarters. Many of the other buildings were torn down in the 1950s *(see p64)*.

City Hall
When opened in 1965, the building, with its two curving towers, was controversial in conservative Toronto; it has since become a much-loved icon of the city's modern architecture *(see p36)*.

Building Feats
One of the seven wonders of the modern world, the CN Tower is recognized as an unparalleled feat of 20th-century engineering. It took 40 months, with 1,537 workers toiling around the clock, to build the tower, pouring enough concrete to lay a sidewalk from Toronto to Kingston, 160 miles (260 km) away. A 10-ton Russian Sikorsky helicopter was used to lift the 44 pieces of the 335-ft (102-m) antenna into place.

Niagara Falls
If the weather cooperates, it's possible to see the mists rising above Niagara Falls, 80 miles (130 km) to the southeast *(see pp28–9)*. The gentle curve of land along the shores of Lake Ontario reveals why the region, which extends from Toronto to Niagara, is known as the Golden Horseshoe.

TOP 10 Toronto Islands

Originally a peninsula, the islands were formed when the rushing waters of the Don River separated a spit from the mainland during a ferocious storm in 1858. There are more than a dozen islets and mid-sized islands in this urban archipelago, some of them connected by bridges, others accessible only by boat. A thriving residential community of creative characters calls Ward's and Algonquin islands home, while Centre Island is a popular destination for its amusement park. No cars are allowed on the islands, adding enormously to their tranquil charm. Along with exploration on foot, two great ways to get the most out of the island experience are to rent a boat or a bicycle and paddle your way through the extensive lagoon system or cycle to a secluded picnic spot. It is easy to forget that you are right beside one of the busiest ports in Canada.

Cottage, Ward's Island

Numerous fast-food spots and snack bars ensure you won't go hungry on the islands. Or bring a picnic lunch.

Ferries depart from the terminal at the foot of Bay Street. Centre Island ferries operate in summer only; Ward's Island and Hanlan's Point ferries, year-round.

The ferry ride ($6.50 round-trip) takes about 10 minutes. Bicycles are permitted on board, except on the Centre Island boat during weekends and holidays, when it can be very busy.

Boat rentals: 416 397 2628

Bicycle rentals: 416 203 0009

- *Map B6–E6*
- *Ferry schedule: 416 392 8193*

Top 10 Features

1. Ferry
2. Boardwalk
3. Ward's Island
4. Gibraltar Point Lighthouse
5. Centreville Amusement Park
6. Far Enough Farm
7. Algonquin Island
8. Hanlan's Point
9. The Rectory
10. Bicycling

1 Ferry

Enjoy one of the best views to be had of the Toronto skyline *(center)* aboard a ferry dating back to the 1950s – some in the fleet even to the 1930s – as it chugs across the lake to the Toronto Islands.

2 Boardwalk

The 1.5-mile (2.5-km) boardwalk runs from Ward's Island to Centre Island and is great for a lakeside stroll *(below)*.

3 Ward's Island

Over 700 people now live here in what began, in the 1880s, as a tiny tent settlement. Stroll along the pathways and marvel at the creative ways the cottages have been ornamented to reflect their owners' tastes. As on neighboring Algonquin Island, the gardens of Ward's Island are in delightful bloom in the warmer months.

For more information on Toronto Islands ferries **See p108**

Toronto City Airport

Toronto Inner Harbour

Ward's Island

Hanlan's Point

Centre Island

Lake Ontario

Gibraltar Point Lighthouse

Toronto's oldest lighthouse *(left)* has served as a shipping beacon since the early 19th century. The historic limestone landmark is rumored to be haunted by the ghost of its first keeper, who disappeared without a trace in 1815.

Centreville Amusement Park

This small amusement park on Centre Island has more than 30 rides, including swan boats *(above)* and a colorful 1890s carousel *(see p49)*.

Far Enough Farm

Kids will love feeding and petting the lambs, goats, cows, geese, pigs, and other farm animals at this small petting zoo.

Algonquin Island

Island residents' creativity is most exuberantly expressed in their quirky, colorful gardens. The green thumb enthusiasts of Algonquin Island are often happy to share their tips with passersby.

The Rectory

This cozy restaurant also functions as Ward's Island informal social center. Main course soups, salads, and sandwiches are healthy and hearty, and the desserts are delicious.

Hanlan's Point

Two sandy beaches, popular with sunbathers, are the big draw here. In 1999, one of the beaches reclaimed its clothing-optional status, which it enjoyed when it first opened in 1894 *(see p51)*.

Bicycling

The best way to tour the islands is on wheels along the pedestrian-bicycle trails stretching the 4-mile (6.5-km) archipelago. Rent a one-person or tandem bike or quadracycle *(right)*.

Canada's Coney Island

The heyday of Hanlan Point began in the 1880s as city dwellers flocked to its vaudeville theater, dance hall, hotels, and amusement park. Two decades later, thousands of fans cheered on baseball great Babe Ruth as he hit his first professional home run, on September 5, 1914, at the Point's new stadium. By 1937, however, the declining resort had been torn down to make way for the Island Airport.

⭐10 Art Gallery of Ontario

Founded in 1900 and now one of the most prominent art museums in North America, the wide-ranging Art Gallery of Ontario (AGO) has over 68,000 works. The outstanding pieces of Canadian art, in particular paintings by the Group of Seven, are a national treasure. Along with superb Henry Moore plasters, bronzes, and other works, the gallery exhibits significant masterpieces of European art, from paintings by Tintoretto and Frans Hals to Vincent van Gogh and Pablo Picasso. A major renovation, designed by architect Frank Gehry, was completed in November 2008. It includes a free contemporary gallery with rotating exhibits, accessible at street level during gallery hours.

The Grange

🍴 The AGO offers a lower level café with a family-friendly light lunch menu and a casual chic restaurant featuring regional Canadian cuisine.

🛍 Browse the Gallery Shop for specialty gifts, reproductions from the gallery's collection, posters, books, and handcrafted jewelry.

Join one of the free tours for extra insight into the collections and exhibits. Call the What's On tour hotline at 416 979 6649 for daily listings.

- *317 Dundas St W*
- *Map J3*
- *416 979 6648*
- *www.ago.net*
- *Open 10am–8:30pm Wed–Fri, 10am–5:30pm Sat, Sun & Tue.*
- *Adm: $18 adults; $10 youths and students; $15 senior citizens; $45 family ticket; under 5s free*

Top 10 Collections

1. The Grange
2. Henry Moore
3. Group of Seven
4. French Impressionists
5. 20th-Century Canadian
6. Contemporary
7. Thomson Collection
8. Prints and Drawings
9. Photography
10. Inuit Art

The Grange
This Georgian mansion was the Art Gallery of Ontario's first home. Restored to the period 1834–40, it gives a taste of what life was like for Toronto's privileged class in the mid-19th century.

Henry Moore
The world's largest public collection of works by British artist Henry Moore (1898–1986) encompasses bronze sculptures, plaster and bronze maquettes, drawings, and prints. His monumental *Large Two Forms (right)* broods outdoors, with its surface now worn smooth by admirers' countless rubbings.

Group of Seven
Iconic scenes of the Canadian landscape epitomize this deeply influential group of painters who strove, in the 1920s, to create a national artistic identity. The collection features signature work by A. Y. Jackson *(center)*, Lawren Harris, and Tom Thomson, who died before the group officially banded together.

➡ *General admission to the gallery is free every Wednesday, 6–8:30pm; a fee may be charged for entrance to some exhibits*

French Impressionists
Claude Monet *(above)*, Camille Pissarro, and Pierre-Auguste Renoir are just some of the 19th-century artists whose masterpieces grace this estimable collection.

5 20th-Century Canadian
Major works by Betty Goodwin, Joanne Tod, and Elizabeth Magor demonstrate the strength and diversity of contemporary Canadian artists. Conceptual art is represented by Michael Snow *(below)*, Jeff Wall, and Paterson Ewen, who painted on plywood gouged with an electric router.

6 Contemporary
Abstract Expressionist, Pop, Minimal, and Conceptual examples illustrate the evolution of late-20th-century art in North America and Europe.

7 Thomson Collection
The largest philanthropic cultural gift in Canadian history, these 2,000 works add remarkable depth to the AGO's collection, with emphasis on Tom Thomson and the Group of Seven, 19th-century painters Cornelius Krieghoff and Paul Kane, and the work of 20th-century radical abstract expressionists Paul-Émile Borduas and Jean-Paul Riopelle.

8 Prints and Drawings
The works in this collection range from the 15th to 21st centuries and include important Italian, Dutch, German, French, and British pieces. *Adam and Eve* (1504) by German etcher Albrecht Dürer *(below)* is a highlight. Works by Canadian artists also have a strong presence. Selected pieces can be viewed in the Marvin Gelber Study Centre.

9 Photography
This broad collection showcases historic calotypes by Linnaeus Tripe and work by 20th-century modernist Josef Sudeck, plus photographs from the 1930s presses. International works round out the collection.

10 Inuit Art
This fine collection of works produced after World War II includes sculptures, prints, and wall hangings crafted from indigenous materials.

The Grange
This elegant Georgian mansion, the city's oldest standing brick house, was built in 1817, when Toronto was just the small town of Muddy York in Upper Canada. The owners, D'Arcy Boulton Jr., and his wife, Sarah Anne, were prominent members of the elite. Their grand home, resembling an English country manor, with a staff of 10, was a focal point of the town's social life. Period furnishings, which include a pianoforte, lap desk, and sleigh bed, occupy the first and second floors of the mansion, while the aroma of bread baking in the 19th-century brick oven wafts through the belowground working kitchen.

Casa Loma

This medieval-style castle, completed in 1914 for a staggering $3.5 million, looms on a hill, overlooking downtown. Designed by famed Toronto architect E. J. Lennox (see p36), Casa Loma – Spanish for "house on the hill" – was the estate of prominent financier and industrialist Sir Henry Pellatt, who was forced by financial ruin to abandon his 98-room dream home less than 10 years after it was built.

Façade detail

🍴 A Druxy's Famous Deli, known for its smoked meat sandwiches, is on the lower level.

🔊 Wander the castle on your own self-guided audio tour, available at no charge in eight languages.

The colorful estate gardens are open May–Oct, with daily tours (2pm) Jul–Aug.

• 1 Austin Terrace
• Map C2
• 416 923 1171
• www.casaloma.org
• Open daily 9:30am–5pm (last admittance 4pm); closed Dec 25 & Jan 1
• Adm: $16 adults; $10 senior citizens and students; $8.75 children aged 4–13

Top 10 Features

1. Tunnel
2. Great Hall
3. Oak Room
4. Sir Henry's Study
5. Sir Henry's Bathroom
6. Conservatory
7. Towers
8. Gardens
9. Library
10. Round Room

◀1▶ Tunnel
Hidden 18 ft (5.5 m) below ground, an 800-ft (240-m) tunnel connects the castle to the carriage house and stables, where Sir Pellatt's horses were kept in grand style: mahogany stalls and floors of Spanish tile were laid in a herring-bone pattern to prevent the horses from slipping.

◀2▶ Great Hall
The grand entrance hall *(below)*, with its 60-ft- (18-m-) high ceiling, sets the castle's tone of splendor. Gargoyles grin down on visitors from the pillars. Audio guide tapes are available here.

◀3▶ Oak Room
It took artisans three years to carve the magnificent French oak paneling in this stately drawing room. The ceiling's lavish plaster moldings conceal indirect lighting – the first time this type of lighting was used in a Canadian home.

◀4▶ Sir Henry's Study
Look closely at the wood panels by the fireplace – they conceal two secret passages. The one to the right gave Sir Henry quick passage to the wine cellar, and his huge wine collection. Climb the one to the left and you'll reach the second floor, near his bedroom suite.

◀5▶ Sir Henry's Bathroom
Heavy on hedonistic comfort, the shower was designed to completely surround the body with sprays of water from above and from the sides, with six large taps controlling three levels of pipes. The walls are made of Carrara marble imported from Italy.

Conservatory

6 Magnificent bronze and glass doors, each costing $10,000, are reproductions of a set made for an Italian villa. The intricate stained-glass ceiling dome, from Italy, was originally backlit by 600 light bulbs so that it glowed at night *(left)*. Beneath the conservatory lies a swimming pool that was never completed.

Towers

7 Stunning views reward those not afraid of heights. The east tower *(above)* is based on Scottish castle design; climb to the top and survey the property from its highest perch. The west tower, of Norman design, offers a breathtaking view of the city.

Gardens

8 Lavish gardens *(left)*, punctuated by sculptures and fountains, grace the estate with bloom during the growing season. Eight themed areas range from formal rose beds to woodland with luscious spring wildflowers. Don't miss the restored Potting Shed, its photo display chronicling the original gardens.

Library

9 Stripes of light and dark wood in the herringbone oak floor create an optical illusion of different shadings from each end of the room *(below)*. The elaborate plaster ceiling decoration features portrait busts and the family's coats of arms.

Round Room

10 With doors and windows custom-bowed to align with the curved walls, this room *(above)* is furnished with period pieces. Sir Pellatt's suite of ornately carved Louis XV chairs and folding screen are upholstered in rare French tapestry.

First in Luxury

As founder of the Toronto Electric Light Company, Sir Henry Pellatt brought electric power to the city, so it is not surprising that his home featured innovations that enhanced comfort on a scale never before seen in a Canadian home. Then-modern conveniences include an electric lighting system controlled from a panel in Sir Henry's bedroom, a central vacuuming system, forced-air heating, and the city's first electric elevator in a private home.

Distillery Historic District

Walking the pedestrian-only cobblestone streets past the best preserved Victorian industrial architecture in North America, you'll feel as if you've stumbled into another century. The 44 buildings of this 13-acre (5-ha) site were, until the mid-1900s, part of Gooderham and Worts, once the world's largest distillery. The distillery evolved from a grist mill founded here in 1832 by Englishman James Wort and his brother-in-law William Gooderham. The 150-year-old district has been infused with new life and is a vibrant community of cafés, restaurants, galleries, art studios, performance venues, and specialty shops.

Gooderham & Worts sign

🍴 **Brick Street Bakery** offers excellent 100-percent-organic breads, meat pies, sandwiches, and desserts for take-away or to enjoy on its picnic tables.

✪ **Stop at the Visitor Centre**, in The Stables (Trinity St at Tank House Lane), for a map and events information.

Join a guided tour ($15), a Segway tour ($39, $69), or rent a self-guided audio tour, available at the Visitor Centre, to get the most out of your visit. Email info@distillery-tours.ca or phone for details.

The district hosts many events, such as jazz and dance festivals (May & Aug) and outdoor art exhibits.

- 55 Mill St
- Map E5
- 416 364 1177
- www.thedistillery district.com

Top 10 Sights

1 Cannery
2 Pure Spirits Building
3 Paint Shop
4 Boiler House Complex
5 Cooperage
6 Case Goods Warehouse
7 Pump House
8 Stone Distillery
9 Molasses Storage
10 Denaturing Room

1 Cannery
Vibrant theater, opera, and dance companies have set up their head-quarters in this building where industrial-grade alcohol was once canned. Perigee restaurant on the second floor serves up an excellent tasting menu from its open kitchen.

2 Pure Spirits Building
Fronted with enormous windows to let in natural light – designed to diminish the fire hazard of producing alcohol under gas lighting – this 1873 building *(above)* is the perfect setting for the several art and photography galleries within.

3 Paint Shop
While many of the Distillery buildings still smell faintly of the grain and alcohol once stored within, this 1879 building *(above)* renews its scent of malt and hops daily, as the Mill Street Brewery. Traditional handcrafted beers include an organic lager and a robust coffee porter. While sipping samples at the bar, check out the display of vintage distilling equipment.

4 Boiler House Complex
In the 1860s, the boiler house heated the entire distillery. Other buildings in the complex housed a carpentry shop, a blacksmith, and a canteen. They have now been converted into two restaurants, including 1832 Pizza and Pasta Bar, with patio seating in summer, and Brick Street Bakery.

Top contemporary Canadian artwork is featured in many of the galleries in the Pure Spirits Building and the Stone Distillery

Plan of Distillery District

Cooperage
Wooden barrels for aging whisky were manufactured here; stenciled instructions to workers are still on the walls. Today, the Sandra Ainsley Gallery *(above)*, exhibits glass art, including lavish sculpture by American Dale Chihuly.

Case Goods Warehouse
The majority of arts organizations and artists in the Distillery complex have their offices, workshops, and studios in this building where cartons of liquor were once stored *(above)*. Many artisans display their unique works, including embroidery, jewelry, and handwoven clothing, in the boutiques here.

Pump House
The pumps in this redbrick building led from the underground water reservoir, in case of fire; others were used for alcohol flow. It's now home to the delightful Balzac's café *(below)*. Beans are roasted Mondays and Fridays.

Stone Distillery
This massive limestone structure is the complex's oldest. Its exterior retains features, such as a winch, from the days when the shoreline – and ships – came right up to the building. Inside are excellent art galleries.

Molasses Storage
Upscale contemporary furniture and home accessory shops, among others, occupy the complex where a huge tank used to store molasses for rum once stood.

Denaturing Room
Machines used by the distillery for alcohol production are dotted throughout the building, as are craft boutiques and specialty food shops.

Filming at the Distillery

When the Gooderham and Worts Distillery ceased operations in 1990, the entire site, with its evocative atmosphere, began a new life as the largest film set outside Hollywood. With hundreds of film shoots here in the past decade, including *Chicago*, *X-Men*, and *The Hurricane*, along with television series such as *La Femme Nikkita* and *Alfred Hitchcock Presents*, this is Canada's busiest filming location.

Visit the farmers' market held every Sunday during July and August on the Distillery District's boardwalk

TOP 10 Ontario Place

This internationally acclaimed cultural, leisure, and entertainment complex, designed by Eb Zeidler (see p24) and opened in 1971, is centered on three man-made islands along the Lake Ontario waterfront. The park is filled with family attractions, from rides to concert venues; snack bars and restaurants are dotted throughout the complex. Taking full advantage of its lakeside setting, Ontario Place offers fantastic water activities, with the city's only downtown waterpark, featuring gigantic waterslides, flume rides, and wading pools for toddlers. The complex is open from late May to late September.

Water fun at Ontario Place

🔴 Hit a snack bar for a beavertail – deep-fried pastry dusted with cinnamon sugar.

🔵 Full-service restaurants offer patios and great lake views.

Buy a Play All Day Pass for unlimited use of most rides for $30.

Check out the Festival Stage for free live children's entertainment.

Molson Amphitheatre box office, at the Main Gate, is open 11am–8pm daily; until event start time on show days. Ticket prices include grounds admission.

• 955 Lake Shore Blvd W
• Map A5
• 416 314 9900
• www.ontarioplace.com
• Open early Jun–Labour Day: 10am daily (closing varies); last 2 weeks in May & 2nd–4th week in Sep: 10am–6pm Sat–Sun
• Adm: $11.75 for grounds; under 3s free

Top 10 Attractions

1 Cinesphere
2 MegaMaze
3 Soak City
4 Pedal Boats
5 Thrill Zone
6 Free Fall
7 Miniature Golf
8 Wilderness Adventure Ride
9 Molson Amphitheatre
10 Go Zone

Cinesphere

With a six-story-high screen and 24,000 watts of digital sound, this IMAX theater *(below)* makes movie-watching a spine-tingling experience. For best viewing, pick a seat in the middle of a row. The theater, housed in a Triodetic dome, was the world's first permanent IMAX venue when it was built, in 1971.

MegaMaze

Navigate seven mazes in this multilevel indoor-outdoor labyrinth. Mirrors, lasers, and sound effects add to the challenge of finding your way out.

Soak City

This waterpark features four heart-stopping rides. The Hydrofuge shoots riders through a tunnel into a giant bowl, where you spin in circles before landing in a pool of water, while the Rush River Raft Ride takes riders on an exhilarating, 873-ft (266-m) plunge. Children who do not meet the age and height restrictions can have lots of wet and wild fun in the splash pool.

For Molson Amphitheatre concert listings, call its concert line at 416 260 5600 or view them online at www.molsonamp.com

West Entrance   Main Entrance

Plan of Ontario Place

Pedal Boats
Rent a pedal boat on Adventure Island to explore the many lagoons and bays. Kids can try the Mini Bumper Boats *(above)*, in Centre Plaza.

Thrill Zone
Three Thrill Zone sites offer the latest in interactive, virtual game hardware. Challenge yourself with Alpine Ski simulators, driving simulators, Wave Jet, Sega Rally, and a large variety of coin-operated video games.

Miniature Golf
Two well-designed nine-hole golf courses built into the landscaped hillside offer great family fun *(below)*.

Molson Amphitheatre
A sensational line-up of international and Canadian musical acts, from rock and hip-hop to country, blues, and jazz, is presented at this large outdoor concert venue.

Go Zone
At this play area, kids can climb the huge H_2O Generation Station, steer electric cars through a realistic course at OP Driving School; and dodge the Atom Blaster's *(left)* 12,000 foam balls, shot in all directions from canons and volcanoes. Microkids is a play area just for toddlers.

Free Fall
Hold on to your hat – and clench your stomach – on this drop tower ride. A platform seating 10 people rises 20 ft (6 m) above the ground before plummeting, for two minutes of hair-raising fun.

Wilderness Adventure Ride
Against a backdrop modeled on the Northern Ontario landscape – deep canyons, forests, and wildlife – this animated flume ride, the world's largest, features a 40 ft (10 m) splashdown.

IMAX
Toronto-based IMAX Corporation is a world leader in large-screen cinema systems. Founded in 1967, the company develops film technologies that heighten the illusory sense of immersion in the cinema experience, including 3-D projections, which simulate a sensation of movement in the viewer. 70mm film stock is used to project an image 10 times the size of conventional 35mm film – what you see in a regular theater. Each IMAX film reel weighs 200 to 300 lbs (90 to 135 kg). A special cooling system in the theater pumps water through the gigantic lamp housing to prevent heat damage to the film. Over 130 venues around the world use IMAX projection systems.

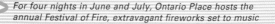

📻10 Eaton Centre

Named after Canadian retail legend Timothy Eaton – whose mail-order catalog and department store, Eaton's, was a beloved national institution until 1999, when the company declared bankruptcy – this multi-story shopping center is the quintessential downtown mall: big, busy, and boisterous. Opened in 1979 and heralded as the anchor that would transform down-at-heel Yonge and Dundas streets into an upscale destination, the complex houses some 300 stores, restaurants, and cafés.

Shoppers

🍴 Grab a quick bite in the concourse food court, or head to the charming Trinity Square Cafe, in the Church of the Holy Trinity, for a good-value soup and sandwich.

🔄 Ride the glass elevators, near the central fountain, for a great view of the galleria.

Navigate PATH using the color-coded signs: the red P steers you south, the orange A west, the blue T north, and the yellow H east.

• 1 Dundas St W (with alternative entrances along Yonge St between Dundas and Queen, and at Queen St west of Yonge St)
• Map L3
• 416 598 8560
• www.torontoeaton centre.com
• Open 10am–9pm Mon–Fri, 9:30am–7pm Sat, noon–6pm Sun; closed Good Friday, Easter Sunday, and Dec 25

Top 10 Attractions

1. Flight Stop
2. Fountain
3. Galleria
4. Yonge-Dundas Square
5. The Labyrinth
6. Church of the Holy Trinity
7. Bronze Plaque
8. PATH
9. The Bay
10. Scadding House

1 Flight Stop
This sculpted gaggle of Canada geese by renowned Toronto artist Michael Snow – so life-like that you almost expect to hear the birds honk – is suspended from the vaulted ceiling of the central atrium.

2 Fountain
A focal point of the Eaton Centre, this water-burst fountain *(below)* lulls with soothing sounds of falling water and then astonishes as water shoots 100 ft (30 m) into the air. Encircled by stone benches, the fountain is a good spot to sit and take a break from shopping.

3 Galleria
Natural light pours through the soaring glass roof into the 865-ft- (265-m-) long arcade *(above)*, which links the mall's two anchor department stores. Designed by Eb Zeidler, architect of Ontario Place *(see pp22–3)*, the galleria is modeled on Milan's 19th-century Galleria Vittoria Emanuele.

4 Yonge-Dundas Square

Toronto's once-tawdry intersection is now a public square *(above)* embellished with 22 fountains set flush to the ground. At its east end, Olympic Spirit Toronto, which is staffed by athletes, offers an exciting variety of simulator games for young and old.

5 The Labyrinth

This circuitous grass path is modeled on the 13th-century labyrinth at Chartres Cathedral in France.

7 Bronze Plaque

This historic plaque commemorates Yonge Street, ranked the longest street in the world by the Guinness Book of World Records. Yonge Street divides East and West Toronto and is the site of the city's first subway line.

9 The Bay

The Bay, founded by Hudson's Bay Company, is Canada's largest department store chain. It sells a wide selection of merchandise, such as home furnishings and fashion, but might be best known for its point blankets, first used in 1670 to barter for beaver pelts with the Cree. Its trading posts, based in the vast north of what is now Canada, were influential centers of commerce.

10 Scadding House

Built in 1857 for the Church of the Holy Trinity's first rector, this Georgian-Gothic house *(right)* was moved here to make way for the mall. The church and house, once surrounded by woodland, may be Yonge St's oldest building complex. The current rector lives in the house.

Plan of Eaton Centre

6 Church of the Holy Trinity

This Anglican church dating to 1847 is as an oasis of calm amid commercial bustle. Admire the turreted entranceway while picnicking on the grounds; step inside to see the stained-glass windows.

8 PATH

From the Eaton Centre you can access the 27-mile (16-km) underground walkway network PATH *(left)*. Linking several major attractions, including the Air Canada Centre and Roy Thompson Hall, PATH winds through a veritable city of stores and food courts.

Hudson's Bay Company (HBC)

For 200 years, HBC controlled North America's lucrative fur trade. It was so powerful that it could make laws and wage war with Native tribes. After years of English-French battles over its posts, HBC lost its monopoly. In 1870, it sold its land to the Government of Canada. Turning to retail, HBC opened its first store in 1881, but kept a hand in the fur trade until 1991, when its last fur salon closed.

Founded in 1670, the Hudson's Bay Company is one of the world's oldest companies

🔟 Hockey Hall of Fame

This shrine to Canada's favorite sport celebrates all things hockey, including those who have achieved greatness in the game. Housed in part in a beautiful former bank building dating to 1885, which is incorporated into BCE Place (see p36), this Hall of Fame contains the most comprehensive collection of hockey artifacts and memorabilia in the world, among them the first Stanley Cup trophy. Interactive exhibits run the gamut from a multimedia trivia game that tests your hockey knowledge to the more physical challenge of playing goalie against a puck-shooting video projection of hockey star Wayne Gretzky.

Hockey Hall of Fame façade

🍽 Many of the eateries in BCE Place *(see p36)* have seating in the spectacular galleria. A food court on the lower level provides quick snacks for those on the go.

🎭 If your energy flags, take a seat in either of the Hall of Fame's two theater venues to watch a retrospective highlights video or an interactive multimedia presentation.

• 30 Yonge St (enter through BCE Place concourse)
• Map L5
• 416 360 7765
• www.hhof.com
• Open Labour Day–mid-Jun: 10am–5pm Mon–Fri, 9:30am–6pm Sat, 10:30am–5pm Sun; late Jun–Labour Day 9:30am–6pm Mon–Sat, 10am–6pm Sun. Holiday hours may vary; call ahead.
• Adm: $13/$9, under 3s free

Top 10 Highlights

1. Stanley Cup
2. Great Hall
3. Be a Player Zone
4. *Our Game*
5. It's Your Call
6. Broadcast Zone
7. Goalie Mask Exhibit
8. Montreal Canadiens Locker Room
9. Bank of Montreal Building
10. Spirit of Hockey Shop

1 Stanley Cup
One of the world's best-known sports trophies, the original Stanley Cup *(above)* is on display here, as is the current one when not with the reigning team. Named for Canada's sixth Governor General, who proposed a yearly challenge cup, it was first presented in 1893.

2 Great Hall
Players and the icons of hockey are celebrated in this 45-ft- (14-m-) high former banking hall. Giants of the game are given their due on the Honoured Members Wall, and all major NHL trophies are on display.

3 Be a Player Zone
On a faux ice rink, complete with arena boards and multimedia scoreboard, visitors can attempt to score a goal against a life-sized video projection of Toronto Maple Leafs goalie Ed Belfour *(below)*. In another rink, it's your turn to play goalie as video images of hockey greats Wayne Gretzky and Mark Messier take real shots.

Not until its inclusion in the 1920 Olympics and the formation of the NHL in 1934 was hockey seen as serious sport rather than recreation

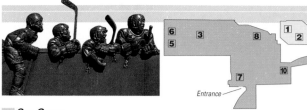

Our Game
Exuberant young players leap over the boards for a hockey game in this larger-than-life bronze sculpture by Ontario artist Edie Parker. Located just outside the museum at the corner of Yonge and Front streets, it is a popular backdrop for photographs.

Key to Floorplan
■ Main Level
■ Upper Level

It's Your Call
For a $2 coin, you can rant or rave on any hockey topic you wish. A video clip of your moment of fame is broadcast on the Hockey Hall of Fame website for 10 days.

Broadcast Zone
Use a high-tech navigational interface – just point and it plays – to custom-design your tour of great moments in hockey broadcast history, from early radio clips to present-day television excerpts. A highlight is the broadcast of the tension-filled last seconds of the 1972 World Summit Series, in which Canada scored on Russia.

Goalie Mask Exhibit
From a leather mask worn in the 1930s to one exemplifying today's sophisticated engineering, this display includes many strange examples of face protection *(right)* that have been personalized by goalies over the years.

Montreal Canadiens Locker Room
The only thing missing from this re-created locker room *(above)* from the old Montreal Forum is the players. Their jerseys and equipment are jumbled about, as if they might swoop in any moment to suit up.

Bank of Montreal Building
Few of the original features of this 1885 rococo beauty are visible inside, but the façade retains its intricate carvings representing human endeavors such as agriculture, music, and industry.

Spirit of Hockey Shop
The museum's exit takes visitors through this shop. Hockey-themed merchandise includes a wide selection of team jerseys, sticks, and smaller items such as mugs and cups emblazoned with logos.

Canada's Game
Although several countries claim to have invented ice hockey, Canada calls the game its own. Even so, its origins are hotly contested. Students at King's College in Windsor, Nova Scotia, are said to have put puck to ice in the early 1800s. Others credit Micmac Indians in Nova Scotia, also in the early 1800s. Whatever the origin, British soldiers stationed at the Halifax, Nova Scotia, garrison were playing the game by the 1850s, as were military men in Kingston, Ontario.

TOP 10 Niagara Falls

One of the world's most famous natural attractions, the great arcs of hissing, frothing water crashing over cliffs 20 stories high is a dazzling spectacle. Drifting spray adds to the excitement of being near the edge of a stomach-churning drop. The 173-ft- (53-m-) high Canadian Horseshoe Falls is the mightiest of the three cataracts that make up Niagara Falls. Across the Niagara River is the impressive American Falls, including the smaller Bridal Veil Falls. When visiting the falls, be sure to make time to stop at some of the other sights in the Niagara region, including its renowned vineyards and historic museums.

Maid of the Mist

🟢 Enjoy stunning views and a wide selection of entrées at the Pinnacle Restaurant in the Minolta Tower (6732 Fallsview Blvd; 1 800 461 2492). The $2 elevator fee includes access to the observation decks.

🟢 Black History Tours highlight the Niagara Freedom Trail, important sites in the stories of 19th-century fugitive slaves (Apr–Nov; call 905 685 5375 for details).

• Map Q3
• www.niagaraparks. com
• Tourist Office: Table Rock Centre; 905 356 2241
• Discount passes available; visit website for details

Top 10 Attractions

1. *Maid of the Mist*
2. Journey Behind the Falls
3. American Falls
4. Horseshoe Falls
5. Whirlpool Rapids
6. Table Rock
7. The Old Scow
8. White Water Walk
9. Butterfly Conservatory
10. Niagara Parks Botanical Gardens

1 Maid of the Mist

Operating since 1846, first as a border-crossing ferry, now as tour boat, the *Maid* gets astonishingly close to the falls. You will be soaked by the end of the 30-minute trip, despite a courtesy raincoat. The thrilling journey goes to the American Falls, then to the foot of the Horseshoe Falls.

2 Journey Behind the Falls

Rock tunnels behind the Horseshoe Falls lead you past a wall of water so thick it blocks out daylight. The vantage point, well below the gorge's rim, is awe-inspiring *(right)*. Rain ponchos are provided – and necessary.

3 American Falls

New York State, on the US side of the international border, lays claim to this cataract, which has a total vertical drop 10 ft (3 m) greater than that of Horseshoe Falls. However, its 950-ft- (290-m-) wide crest and 2-ft (0.6-m) depth sees only a fraction of the volume of water that the Horseshoe Falls carries. It is easily seen from Table Rock.

4 Horseshoe Falls

This 2,625-ft- (800-m-) wide, 20-story cataract is formed as 90 percent of the water of the Niagara River, the natural outlet from Lake Erie to Lake Ontario, roars over a semi-circular cliff of the Niagara Escarpment *(above)*. Water tumbles some 10 ft (3 m) deep at the falls' center.

Brightly colored lights illuminate the falls during the spectacular Winter Festival of Lights (mid-Nov–mid-Jan)

Whirlpool Rapids
A sharp turn in the river just downstream of the falls creates a raging whirlpool, one of the most lethal stretches of water in North America. Daredevils can look down on the rapids from the Whirlpool Aero Car *(above)*, a 1913 cablecar traversing the shores.

Butterfly Conservatory
The butterfly conservatory is a huge heated dome with thousands of colorful creatures *(above)* flitting freely about – and sometimes landing on delighted visitors.

Niagara Parks Botanical Gardens
These beautiful gardens, located 6 miles (9 km) from the falls, include a splendid rose display that features more than 2,000 varieties.

Table Rock
Stand mere feet from the brink of Horseshoe Falls, a rail the only thing between you and a torrent of water. The lookout point was so named because its surface extended above the gorge like a table leaf. Deemed unstable in 1935, the ledge was blasted off.

The Old Scow
Stranded on rocks mid-river is this barge, shipwrecked in 1918. The two-man crew survived but had to wait 29 hours near the brink of the falls before being winched to safety. The best view is on an aerial tour *(see p31).*

White Water Walk
Descend from the top of the chasm by elevator to a tunnel leading to a riverside boardwalk *(below)*. The whirlpools and rapids here are some of the most spectacular, and treacherous, in the world.

Forceful Flow
The forces of erosion that created the falls today wear them away. Before hydroelectric stations were built on the Niagara River, the rock face eroded by up to 6 ft (1.8 m) a year. Now it is just 1 ft (30 cm) annually. Almost a fifth of the Earth's freshwater flows over the falls – so much that it would take only an hour to fill a ditch running between Canada's east and west coasts.

Left **Fort George** Right **Casino Niagara**

Fun Things to Do Around Niagara

Fort George
This historic British fort, built in 1796, was a key defense post during the War of 1812 between Britain and the US *(see p64)*. It has been restored to the period with replica buildings and costumed staff. ◈ *Niagara-on-the-Lake • Map Q3 • Open Apr–Oct: 10am–5pm daily • Adm*

Casino Niagara
Those looking for a different kind of thrill at the falls can test their skill and luck at 3,000 slot machines and more than 100 gaming tables. ◈ *5705 Falls Ave, Niagara Falls • 1 888 946 3255 • Open 24 hrs daily*

Queenston Heights Park
A large monument pays tribute to General Brock, a leader of the British forces killed in battle here during the War of 1812 *(see p64)*. With great views of Niagara River, the park is a fine picnic spot. ◈ *Niagara River Pkwy, Niagara Falls*

IMAX Theatre Niagara Falls
Don't miss the awe-inspiring *Niagara: Miracles, Myths and Magic*, chronicling the history of the falls. Projected onto a giant screen, the movie, thanks to a special filming technique, makes you feel like you're right in the midst of things. Original stunt barrels are displayed in the theater's Daredevil Gallery. ◈ *6170 Fallsview Blvd, Niagara Falls • 905 358 3611*

Skylon Tower
Its viewing deck affording vistas of as far as 80 miles (130 km), this tower rises 775 ft (236 m) above the falls. Fine dining at the revolving restaurant. ◈ *5200 Robinson St • 905 356 2651 • Open summer: 8am–midnight daily; winter: 11am–9pm daily • Adm*

Skylon Tower

Welland Canal
Linking Lakes Ontario and Erie, this eight-lock, 27-mile (43-km) canal first opened in 1829, allowing vessels to traverse the Niagara Escarpment – and the 328 ft (100 m) height difference between the lakes. The canal-side trail from Thorold to St. Catharines is great for ship-gazing. ◈ *Lock 3 Viewing Complex & Museum: Government Rd, St. Catharines • Map Q3 • 1 800 305 5134*

Clifton Hill
This is Niagara Fall's shopping and entertainment district: museums, mini-golf, and midway are just the start. Hotels and restaurants for every budget are also to be found here. ◈ *Niagara Falls*

Ship passing through Welland Canal

Visit Ripley's Believe It or Not! Museum (4960 Clifton Hill; 905 356 2238) to see historic film footage of death-defying stunts

Top 10 Niagara Daredevils

1. Jean Francois Gravelot, aka The Great Blondin, tightrope crossing, 1859
2. Guillermo Antonio Farini, aka The Great Farini, stilt tightrope crossing, 1864
3. Henry Bellini, tightrope crossing and leap into river, 1873
4. Maria Spelterini, first woman to cross on a tightrope, 1876
5. Carlisle Graham, first man over the falls in a barrel, 1886
6. Clifford Calverly, fastest tightrope crossing, 1887
7. Samuel J. Dixon, hung from rope with one hand, 1890
8. James Hardy, youngest tightrope crosser, 1896
9. Annie Edson Taylor, first woman over the falls in a barrel, 1901
10. Lincoln Beachy, first airplane stunt at falls, 1911

Daredevil Feats

For some 200 years, daredevils have risked their lives at Niagara Falls for a chance at fame. Nineteen have died; many others have had close calls. The first daredevil, Sam Patch, dove headfirst from an 85-ft (26-m) -high platform into the churning Niagara River, in 1829, and survived. Ten days later he did it again, from a height of 130 ft (40 m). The Great Blondin couldn't get enough of the falls, crossing the gorge on a tightrope nine times in 1859 – once carrying his manager. When Blondin returned in 1860 for more stunts, such as pushing a wheelbarrow across the rope, he was challenged by a young upstart, The Great Farini, who crossed carrying a washing machine. Farini performed biweekly, becoming increasingly daring – doing headstands, hanging by his toes. He survived them all and died at age 91. The first woman funambulist, Maria Spelterini, also crossed blindfolded, in 1876. The first person to survive going over the falls in a barrel was Annie Taylor, in 1901. Emerging from her battered vessel, the 63-year-old schoolteacher said, "Nobody ought ever do that again," advice dozens have since ignored.

The Great Blondin
Blondin's 1859 tightrope crossing of the Niagara River, his manager on his back

Niagara Helicopter Tour

Experience some 10 minutes of exhilaration as you swoop over whirlpool rapids, then get up close to the falls. ✆ *Niagara Helicopters, 905 357 5672; Skyway, 1 800 491 3117*

Old Fort Erie

This reconstructed fort, a supply base for British troops in the 1700s, was the site of many battles with US forces in the 1800s. ✆ *350 Lakeshore Rd, Ft Erie • Map Q3 • 905 871 0540 • Open mid-May–Sep: 10am–6pm daily; limited hrs Oct • Adm*

MarineLand

Killer whales and arctic belugas aren't the only attractions at this theme park, though to many they are the highlight. Walruses and sea lions also make appearances in the marine animal shows; habitats harbor bear, elk, and deer. Adventurers can hop on the 10-plus rides, including the world's largest looping roller coaster and the only one with a bowtie inversion. ✆ *7657 Portage Rd, Niagara Falls • 905 356 9565 • Open 10am–5pm or later, late May–mid-Oct • Adm*

*Niagara is known for its top vineyards **See p100**; most offer tours, tastings, and wines for sale. For details, visit www.wineroute.com*

Left **Ontario Science Centre** Right **McMichael Canadian Art Collection**

TOP 10 **Museums & Art Galleries**

1 Art Gallery of Ontario
Reflecting some 600 years of human creative endeavor, the gallery's permanent collection contains more than 68,000 works in all media. The Canadian collection is particularly impressive *(see pp16–17)*.

2 Royal Ontario Museum
Canada's foremost museum offers an excellent balance of art, archeology, science, and nature, and has more than six million artifacts in its collections *(see pp8–11)*.

3 Ontario Science Centre
Over 800 high-tech, interactive exhibits within 11 specially themed exhibition halls aim to make science fun and fascinating. Youthful visitors can navigate their way in a rocket chair, climb the rockwall, touch a tornado, and explore the hair-raising effects of electricity *(see p91)*.

4 Gardiner Museum of Ceramic Art
The only museum in North America devoted solely to ceramics was founded in 1984 by private Canadian collectors George and Helen Gardiner to showcase their extraordinary collection of pre-Columbian American pottery and European porcelain. Recent additions include Asian ceramics and contemporary artwork *(see p76)*.

5 Design Exchange
Located in the magnificent former Toronto Stock Exchange building, an Art Deco gem built in 1937, this center celebrates postwar Canadian design. Furniture, housewares, sportsgear, and medical equipment are among the items in the permanent collection and highlight the role of design in daily life. The center also hosts major national and international exhibitions. A gorgeous mural on the upstairs Trading Floor depicts Canadian industrial themes *(see p66)*.

Robe, Textile Museum

6 Textile Museum of Canada
A permanent collection of over 10,000 fabrics, quilts, ceremonial cloths, and carpets from around the world are housed in this small but excellent museum. Temporary contemporary exhibits round out the historical artifacts.
🕾 55 Centre Ave • Map K3 • 416 599 5321 • Open 11am–5pm daily; (until 8pm Wed) • Adm • www.textile museum.ca

7 McMichael Canadian Art Collection
The outstanding Group of Seven collection is the treasure of this gallery. The Group endeavored, in the early 20th century, to express a distinctive national identity through their paintings of the Canadian wilderness *(see p91)*.

 Previous pages **Participants in the International Carnival parade**

Power Plant Contemporary Art Gallery

Known for its boundary-pushing exhibitions of contemporary Canadian and international art, this edgy, non-collecting gallery features rotating shows of consistently high quality. If the art sometimes mystifies visitors, at least the building is instantly recognizable: a brick smokestack tops the 1920s converted power station *(see p66)*.

Toronto Dominion Gallery of Inuit Art

As Inuit tool makers turned their skills to sculpting, the culture experienced a renaissance, this time in artistic achievement. Most of the 200 pieces in this gallery specializing in postwar Inuit sculpture are carved soapstone, each evocative of the landscape, culture, and legends of the indigenous people of Canada's harsh Arctic region. The gallery's design echoes that of the TD Bank Tower, by renowned modernist architect Mies van der Rohe *(see p66)*.

Bata Shoe Museum

This unusual building, resembling a stylized shoebox, houses more than 10,000 shoes, covering 4,500 years of footwear history. Artifacts represent an unparalleled range, from Ancient Egyptian funerary shoes (1500 BC) to 19th-century Nigerian camel-riding boots to Marilyn Monroe's red leather pumps *(see p74)*.

Bata Shoe Museum

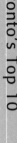

Top 10 Small Museums

1 Gibson House Museum
Elegant 1851 Georgian farmhouse *(see p92)*.

2 Mackenzie House
Home of Toronto's first mayor (1834) *(see p83)*.

3 Toronto's First Post Office
A historic museum and working post office *(see p84)*.

4 Ydessa Hendeles
World-class collection of works by international contemporary artists. § 778 King St W • Map B4 • 416 413 9400 • Open noon–5pm Sat • Adm

5 MOCCA
Toronto's newest museum promotes innovative works. § 952 Queen St W • Map B4 • 416 395 0067 • Free

6 Redpath Sugar Museum
Next door to a refinery, it tells the history of sugar production. § 95 Queens Quay E • Map M6 • 416 366 3561 • Closed Sat, Sun

7 Campbell House
Oldest remaining building (1822) in the city *(see p75)*.

8 University of Toronto Art Centre
Works by Picasso and Matisse, tucked in University College. § 15 King's College Circle • Map J1 • 416 978 1838 • Free

9 Toronto Police Museum and Discovery Centre
Interactive displays, fascinating police artifacts, and exhibits chronicling infamous crimes. § 40 College St • Map L2 • 416 808 7020 • Free

10 CBC Museum
Celebrates the people and programs of Canada's national broadcaster. § 250 Front St W • Map J5 • 416 205 5574 • Free

Left **Union Station** Right **Trinity College, University of Toronto**

🔟 Architectural Highlights

1 BCE Place

Spanish architect Santiago Calatrava designed the striking atrium of this 1990 office complex. Its steel-and-glass canopy creates enchanting patterns of light and shadow. Façades of 19th-century buildings have been preserved in the Yonge Street frontage. ⚲ *181 Bay St • Map L5*

2 Toronto-Dominion Centre

Two austere, perfectly proportioned towers and a single-story pavilion of glass and black metal, all set on a broad plaza, are Toronto's only design by International Style architect Ludwig Mies van der Rohe (1886–1969). Built between 1964 and 1971, the complex spurred the skyscraper boom that gave birth to the city's financial district. Four more towers were later added *(see p64)*.

3 CN Tower

Defining the skyline, Toronto's most recognizable architectural icon is also the world's tallest free-standing structure *(see pp12–13)*.

4 University of Toronto

Founded in 1827 as King's College, this institute has many refined, stately buildings, such as the Romanesque Revival-style University College *(see p76)*.

5 City Hall

Causing a significant stir in 1960s Toronto, the design of New City Hall is bold, daring, and unique. Finnish architect Viljo Revell's two curving towers seem to embrace the central domed structure between them. A sweeping public plaza out front, Nathan Phillips Square, is the symbolic heart of the city *(see p75)*.

City Hall

6 Old City Hall

Now a courthouse, this Richardsonian Romanesque building, completed in 1899, was designed by the architect responsible for many of Toronto's grandest historic buildings, E. J. Lennox. For the best view of the clock tower, look north up Bay Street *(see p76)*.

Old City Hall

Dozens of architecturally significant buildings invite in the public every May during Doors Open Toronto; visit www.doorsopen.org

Sharpe Centre for Design

7 Sharpe Centre for Design
Propped up on 100-ft (30-m) stilts, British architect Will Alsop's addition to the Ontario College of Art and Design is playful and audacious. The two-story "table-top" building connects to the main building via a sloping tunnel. ✪ 100 McCaul St • Map J3

8 Royal Bank Plaza
The 14,000 mirrored windows of the two towers (1977) are insulated with 24-karat gold – $70 worth on each window, for a total of some $1 million, money saved on heating. ✪ 200 Bay St • Map K4

9 Ontario Legislative Building
The best view of this massive Richardsonian Romanesque building (1892), the seat of provincial government, is from College Street, looking north past the expanse of lawn. Built on the former site of a lunatic asylum (political pundits take note), the richly carved exterior is matched by the ornate interior (see p76).

10 Union Station
The Great Hall of this 1920s monumental stone railroad station has an 88-ft- (27-m-) high vaulted ceiling (see p66).

Top 10 Public Art Sites

1 The Pasture
Joe Fafard's seven bronze, life-size cows in gentle repose. ✪ 77 King St W • Map L4

2 Three Way Piece No. 2
Aka The Archer, this Henry Moore bronze, controversial when installed in 1966, is now a local favorite. ✪ Nathan Phillips Sq • Map K3

3 Wall and Chairs
Curved walls intersected by a triangle of three chairs echo the severe beauty of city towers. ✪ TD Centre • Map K4

4 Toronto Sculpture Garden
Rotating exhibits of contemporary site-specific works. ✪ 115 King St E • Map L4

5 Elevated Wetlands
Don River water is recycled as it filters through plants atop large white bearlike forms. ✪ Taylor Creek Park • Map F1

6 Search Light, Star Light, Spot Light
Three hollow metal columns are pierced by hundreds of stars; lit from within, they glow like searchlights. ✪ Air Canada Centre • Map K5

7 Untitled (Mountain)
A gorgeously layered aluminum sculpture, cut with water jets, by Anish Kapoor. ✪ Simcoe Park • Map J4

8 The Audience
Boisterous "fans" spill out of the SkyDome in this frieze by Michael Snow. ✪ Map J5

9 Woodpecker Column
Woodpeckers strike at a 100-ft (30-m) column. ✪ 222 Bremner Blvd • Map J5

10 City People
Colorful aluminum figures spin softly in the breeze. ✪ Royal Bank Plaza • Map K4

Left **Boardwalk, The Beach** Right **Cabbagetown**

Neighborhoods

1 The Beach
A charming enclave east of Woodbine Ave full of fun for the outdoor enthusiast, including those who consider shopping a sport. Browse the eclectic shops or relax in one of the many cozy restaurants or pubs *(see p93)*. Just south of the Queen Street East strip, a popular board-walk stretches alongside a sandy beach to Ash-bridges Bay *(see p40)*.

2 Chinatown
With the largest ethnic Chinese popu-lation of any North American city, it's not surprising that Toronto has several Chinatowns, though none other as old as this one, settled in the early 1900s. Original-ly farther east on Dundas Street, the hub is now Spadina Avenue, where scores of shops and restaurants – including many Viet-namese ones – rub shoulders. The area is even more frenetic during Chinese New Year celebrations, usually in February *(see p73)*.

Chinatown signs

3 Cabbagetown
Settled in the 1840s by hardscrabble Irish immigrants who grew cabbages in their front gardens to help make ends meet, this area east of Sher-bourne St between Wellesley St E and

Gerrard St E is today almost com-pletely gentrified. Picturesque cottages and Victorian rowhouses with their lovely gardens are rich in vernacular architectural history, rewarding exploration *(see p83)*.

4 Little Italy
Most of the 500,000 Italians who call Toronto home now live north of the city, but the pizzerias, and *trattorias* that remain on this once pre-dominantly Italian strip of College St west of Bathurst St ensure it retains its flair. At night, music and patrons spill out of trendy bars and restaurants *(see p76)*.

5 Yorkville
Famous in the 1960s as a hip-pie hangout and now the city's most exclusive retail district, this window-shoppers' paradise abounds with eye-candy. Refined art galleries nestle among chic boutiques, bars, and restaurants. Visiting movie stars can often be spotted here, especially during film festival time *(see p74)*.

Yorkville

Toronto's smaller downtown Chinatown is at Broadview Avenue and Gerrard Street, on the city's east side

6 The Danforth

This is the social and commercial heart of Greek and Macedonian life in Toronto. At night, especially between Chester St and Pape Ave, lively tavernas are crowded with patrons enjoying souvlaki and seafood, accompanied by *retsina* or *ouzo*. In the day, shops are the draw *(see p83)*.

7 The Annex

This upscale neighborhood is home to students, families, and professionals. Huge trees front the Edwardian houses. Bloor St, a main traffic artery, is lined with shops between Bathurst Ave and Spadina Ave selling inexpensive clothing, jewelry, books, and secondhand CDs, and with eateries that won't tax your wallet, including many ethnic and vegetarian spots. On weekends, the streets and bars are filled with young revelers *(see p76)*.

8 Roncesvalles

Toronto's Polish community lays claim to this west-end neighborhood. Its heart, Roncesvalles Ave between Howard Park Ave and Queen St W, is lined with great Polish delis and bakeries (try the jam donuts). Increasingly gentrifying as the ethnic population ages and moves on and young professionals move in, the area still has a working-class feel and Polish is still spoken in shops and on the street.

HONEY BALLS · FAMOUS BAKLAVA · CUSTARD CREAM
ALMOND COOKIES · SAMALI · FRESH DAILY BREAD

Greek shop on The Danforth

9 Leslieville

One of the newer areas of Toronto to take shape as a destination, what this district lacks in architectural richness it makes up for in character. Along Queen St E between Carlaw Ave and Leslie St, secondhand furniture, housewares, and vintage stores offer 1960s and 1970s bric-a-brac, though you might have to compete with the set designers from the nearby film studios for the object of your desire. Casual cafés are perfect for weekend brunches and several good restaurants have opened up here. ❧ *Map F4*

10 Little India

The festive spirit of the market bazaars of the Indian subcontinent is alive and well – even during Toronto's cold winter – on Gerrard St E between Greenwood Ave and Coxwell Ave. Shops sell colorful saris, street vendors cook up tantalizing takeaway, and restaurants serve excellent Indian fare, from vegetarian *masala dosa* to *halwa*, a carrot-based sweet.

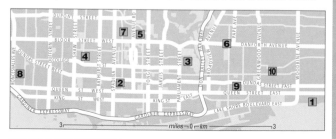

Left **Leslie Street Spit** Right **High Park**

🔟 Greenspaces

1 Leslie Street Spit

Also known as Tommy Thompson Park – after Toronto's first commissioner of parks and the official who peppered them with welcoming "Please Walk on the Grass" signs – this secluded nature reserve is a man-made peninsula extending 3 miles (5 km) into Lake Ontario. More than 290 bird species have been observed in this prime wildlife viewing spot, and its wetlands, meadows, and forests contain many rare and unusual plants. The lighthouse at the southern tip is a common destination for bicyclists. ✆ Map F6

2 Don Valley Brickworks

Nature has reclaimed the quarry of this historic former brickworks: the ponds and meadows of what is now known as Weston Quarry Gardens attract birds and wildlife. Stop by the world-famous excavated "wall" to marvel at the fossils of Toronto's early flora and fauna and the region's geologic history; some of its many layers of deposits are over one million years old (see p85).

3 High Park

Several miles of bicycle and walking trails meander through formal gardens, wooded ravines, and a rare oak savanna habitat in downtown's largest park. At the south end is Colborne Lodge (see p92) and Grenadier Pond, where locals fish in summer and skate in winter (see p94).

4 Ashbridges Bay Park

Enjoy a picnic at this lakeside park while watching boats moor, or play a game at the rugby pitch or baseball diamond. At the north end, the Martin Goodman bicycle trail (see p94) meets the Beach boardwalk (see p38).

5 Mount Pleasant Cemetery

The array of trees – many magnificently old and stately – in this cemetery dating from 1876 qualifies it as a bona fide arboretum. A walk through the lovely grounds will reveal the graves of several notable Canadians, including pianist Glenn Gould (1932–82), whose marker is carved with the opening bars of J. S. Bach's Goldberg Variations. ✆ Map D1

Don Valley Brickworks

➤ Enjoy a Shakespeare play under the stars on the grassy slopes of High Park's amphitheater (Jul–Aug); call CanStage at 416 367 8243

Yorkville Park

Yorkville Park

6 This gem packs a lot of punch within its compact borders. It is elegantly divided into zones, each with a different theme, such as aspen grove, wetland, and meadow. Jets of mist rise at intervals around conifers; the enormous chunk of Canadian Shield granite makes a perfect perch for summer sunning. ® *Map C3*

Humber Bay Park East

7 Views of the city don't get much better than those from here. Easily accessible by bicycle on the Waterfront Trail, the park is also great for exploring on foot. Major habitat restoration such as wildflower meadow plantings attracts birds and butterflies *(see p94)*. Walkways and interpretive signs complement a series of interesting stormwater cleansing ponds. ® *Map A2*

Toronto Music Garden

8 One of the city's most unusual gardens, each of its six sections is inspired by a movement in J.S. Bach's *First Suite for Unaccompanied Cello*. The cumulative effect of swirling paths, undulating hills, and secretive groves is dazzling *(see p65)*.

Rouge Park

9 The largest North American park in an urban area – over 31 sq miles (50 sq km) – borders the Rouge River and its tributaries at the city's eastern edge. It is home to a unique diversity of wildlife and plants, including the best remaining example of a lakeshore marsh in Toronto. You can easily spend a day exploring the trails, either on foot or bicycle *(see p94)*.

Edwards Gardens

10 Marvelous flowerbeds showcasing roses, rhododendrons, and much more make this formal oasis very popular in summer, when wedding parties crowd the manicured lawns for photographs. The Teaching Garden lets kids explore an alphabet of plants and learn hands-on about nature. The Toronto Botanical Garden, a horticultural center, is also here *(see p94)*.

Edwards Gardens

Left **Young swimmers at a public pool** Right **In-line skating on the Martin Goodman Trail**

Outdoor Activities

Swimming
Cherry Beach in the east and Hanlan's Point *(see p15)* are two of Toronto's best beaches. While the city has improved water quality, beaches are often posted with no-swimming signs, often after heavy rains. More reliable are the public pools. *Beaches hotline: 416 392 7161 • Beach and pool info: www.toronto.ca*

Skating
Among Toronto's free outdoor rinks are Nathan Phillips Square *(see p75)* and Harbourfront's Natrel Rink. Both have skate rentals. *Public skating: 416 338 7465 • Natrel Rink: 235 Queens Quay W, Map K6, 416 973 4866*

In-Line Skating
Daring in-line skaters take to the streets, but recreational rollers head to the lake-hugging Martin Goodman Trail *(see p94)*.

Jogging
Extensive park and ravine trails mean lots of choice. Head to the Beach boardwalk *(see p38)*, High Park *(see p40)*, or the more secluded paths by the Don River.

Cycling
Many major roads and parks have bike lanes. A terrific recreational cycle is on the Martin Goodman Trail *(see p94)* or at Leslie Street Spit *(see p40)*.

Cyclist

Hiking
Toronto Field Naturalists (TFN) offer daily tours of natural areas, led by knowledgeable volunteers. The 500-mile (800-km) Bruce Trail, running along the Niagara Escarpment from Niagara to Tobermory, has many access points. The Bruce Trail Association (BTA) is a mine of information. *TFN: 416 593 2656 • BTA: 1 800 665 4453, www.brucetrail.org*

Sailing on Toronto Harbour

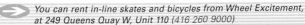
You can rent in-line skates and bicycles from Wheel Excitement, at 249 Queens Quay W, Unit 110 (416 260 9000)

Skating at Nathan Phillips Square, City Hall

Windsurfing and Sailing
You can take windsurfing lessons or rent a board by joining the Toronto Windsurfing Club at Cherry Beach, the city's best surfing spot. Sailors can choose from four public marinas – the largest at Bluffer's Park *(see p94)* – or a number of private ones *(see p107)*. ✆ *Toronto Windsurfing Club: 416 461 7078* • *Bluffer's Park Marina: 416 266 7808*

Canoeing and Kayaking
The Toronto Islands' lagoons are ideal for paddling; rent a canoe on Centre Island or the mainland at Harborfront Canoe & Kayak Centre, which also offers one-evening classes and local outings. ✆ *Harbourfront Canoe & Kayak Centre: 283A Queens Quay W* • *416 203 2277*

Golfing
The famous Glen Abbey is just 30 minutes west of Toronto; there are also five golf courses in the city. ✆ *Glen Abbey: 1333 Dorval Dr, Oakville; 905 844 1811* • *Tam O'Shanter Golf Course: 416 392 2547*

Skiing
Within city limits, at North York Ski Centre and Centennial Park, are only small hills; two hours north of Toronto, at Collingwood, is Ontario's best skiing *(see p98)*. Phone the city's ski hotline for details. ✆ *Ski hotline: 416 338 6754*

Top 10 Spectator Sports

1 Toronto Maple Leafs
This NHL team inspires hometown adoration. ✆ *Air Canada Centre, 40 Bay St* • *416 703 5323*

2 Toronto Blue Jays
Member of Major League baseball's American League. ✆ *Rogers Centre, 1 Blue Jays Way* • *416 341 1234, 1-888-OK-GO-JAY*

3 Toronto Raptors
NBA team that delights fans from November to May. ✆ *Air Canada Centre, 40 Bay St* • *416 872 5000*

4 Toronto Argonauts
Canadian Football League team. ✆ *Rogers Centre, 1 Blue Jays Way* • *416 872 5000*

5 Toronto Rock
Players of lacrosse, the country's official national sport. ✆ *Air Canada Centre, 40 Bay St* • *416 872 5000*

6 Toronto Football Club
Pro-team soccer. ✆ *BMO Field Exhibition Grounds* • *416 360 4625*

7 Woodbine Race Track
Home of the Queen's Plate horse race. ✆ *555 Rexdale Blvd* • *416 675 7223*

8 Molson Indy
Canadian highlight of the CART motor racing series draws crowds to Exhibition Place. ✆ *416 922 7477, 1-877-865-RACE*

9 Toronto Marathon
The 26-mile- (41-km-) race starts at Mel Lastman Square and ends at Queen's Park; mid-October. ✆ *416 972 1062*

10 Toronto Marlies
The AHL team sends players to the NHL. ✆ *Ricoh Coliseum, Exhibition Grounds* • *416 597 7825*

Left **Molson Amphitheatre** Right **Air Canada Centre**

Entertainment Venues

1 Molson Amphitheatre
With its lakeside setting in Ontario Place *(see pp22–3)*, this is a great place to take in a summer concert. There's seating for 9,000 under the copper canopy, plus space for 7,000 on the grass. Top performers often mean sold-out shows. *909 Lake Shore Blvd W • Map A5 • 416 260 5600*

2 Roy Thomson Hall
The concert hall's innovative design ensures that everyone in the audience is within 100 ft (30 m) of the stage *(see p13)*. It is home to the Toronto Symphony Orchestra (which performs September to June) and Toronto Mendelssohn Choir, and also hosts many guest artists. *60 Simcoe St • Map J4 • 416 872 4255 • www.masseyhall.com*

Roy Thompson Hall

3 St. Lawrence Centre for the Arts
This venerable Toronto venue presents theater, dance, and music, along with lectures on subjects of topical interest, in its two intimate spaces. The Canadian Stage Theatre Company is based in the larger Bluma Appel Theatre, while Jane Mallet Theatre features recitals and performances by groups such as the Toronto Operetta Theatre Company. *27 Front St E • Map L5 • 416 366 7723 • www.stlc.com*

4 The Sony Centre
It was here that famed dancer Mikhail Baryshnikov defected from the Soviet Union in 1979. The now refurbished theater mounts shows by the National Ballet of Canada, and others. *1 Front St E • Map L5 • 416 393 7469 • www.sonycentre.ca*

5 Air Canada Centre
When hockey's Maple Leafs and basketball's Raptors are not filling the seats with Toronto fans, the arena hosts big-name musical acts *(see p66)*. *www.theaircanadacentre.com*

6 Rogers Centre
This mega-stadium's retractable roof allows games to be played whatever the weather may be. The arena seats almost 52,000 sports fans, who turn out to see the Blue Jays play baseball or the Argonauts play football on home turf, and holds up to 70,000 concert-goers *(see p63)*. *www.rogerscentre.com*

Rogers Centre

Winter Garden Theatre

7 Elgin and Winter Garden Theatres

These two theaters have been restored to their original splendor. Opened in 1913 as a double-decker venue – the Winter Garden seven stories above the Elgin – they host concerts, operas, and hit Broadway musicals *(see p68)*.

8 Massey Hall

This grand dame of entertainment venues, opened in 1894, was the first dedicated music hall in Toronto with the stage space to accommodate large musical groups. Its 2,700 seats and superb acoustics provide a surprisingly intimate setting for jazz, blues, and folk shows; the Art Deco interior provides all the distraction you'll need at intermission. ⊗ *178 Victoria St • Map L4 • 416 872 4255 • www.masseyhall.com*

9 George Weston Recital Hall

This 1,036-seat concert hall hosts international performers along with local favorites the Toronto Philharmonia and the Amadeus Choir. ⊗ *5040 Yonge St • Map B1 • 416 733 9388 • www.tocentre.com*

10 Glenn Gould Studio

CBC, Canada's national broadcaster, records for-radio musical performances, from classical to jazz, in this small studio named after the famous concert pianist. ⊗ *250 Front St W • Map J5 • 416 205 5555 • http://glenngouldstudio.cbc.ca*

Top 10 Performing Arts Groups

1 Canadian Opera Company
The largest producer of opera in Canada stages seven productions each season.

2 Tarragon Theatre
New innovative works by Canadian playwrights.

3 Tafelmusik Baroque Orchestra and Chamber Choir
The ensemble plays Baroque chamber music on period instruments.

4 Theatre Passe Muraille
A pioneering theater instrumental in shaping a distinctly Canadian voice.

5 Toronto Mendelssohn Choir
Canada's oldest vocal ensemble presented its first concert in 1895.

6 Toronto Symphony Orchestra
This world-renowned orchestra delights audiences with the classics.

7 Canadian Stage Company
Theatrical productions of international and Canadian works, including musicals.

8 National Ballet of Canada
Internationally acclaimed company dances the classics with luster, and presents vibrant new choreography.

9 Toronto Dance Theatre
Intelligent and visually striking modern dance by one of the country's most influential dance troupes.

10 Soulpepper Theatre Company
Canadian interpretations of international classics.

Tours of the Elgin and Winter Garden theaters are offered year-round **See p68;** *visit their website at www.heritagefdn.on.ca*

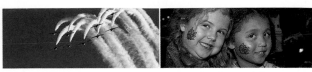

Left **Airshow, Canadian National Exhibition** Right **Children celebrating Canada Day**

🔟 Family Events

1 Canadian National Exhibition

The "Ex" is an 18-day extravaganza with 65 rides on a frenetic midway, themed pavilions, performers of all kinds – from musicians to dancers to jugglers – nightly fireworks, and a dazzling international airshow starring the world-renowned Canadian Air Force Snowbirds. ⚐ *Exhibition Pl • Map A5 • mid-Aug–Labour Day*

2 Canada Day

This national holiday observes the anniversary of the founding of Canada, in 1867. Festivities include free concerts at Nathan Phillips Square and Queen's Park. ⚐ *Jul 1*

3 Festival Caravan

Toronto's multiculturalism is celebrated under one roof at the Metro Convention Centre, each pavilion representing a different culture. Dancing, music, food, and more. ⚐ *Metro Convention Centre: 255 Front St W • Map J5 • Oct • 416 585 8134*

4 Royal Agricultural Winter Fair

North America's largest indoor exhibition of agriculture features all manner of farm animals and products. Horticulture and equestrian shows, and then some. ⚐ *Exhibition Pl • Map A5 • early Nov*

5 Toronto International Carnival

What began as Caribana, a local celebration of Caribbean culture, is now North America's largest street festival, as revelers enjoy island food to rhythmic beats. The highlight is the parade along Lake Shore Blvd: costumed dancers strut their stuff to soca, played by exuberant steel bands atop colorful floats. ⚐ *late Jul*

Carnival costume

6 Milk International Children's Festival

You'll find family entertainment galore at this mainly free festival for kids. Performances of dance, music, theater, and puppetry will enchant the wee ones. ⚐ *Harbourfront • mid-May*

Horse show, Royal Agricultural Winter Fair

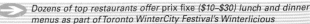

Dozens of top restaurants offer prix fixe ($10–$30) lunch and dinner menus as part of Toronto WinterCity Festival's Winterlicious

Toronto WinterCity Festival

Top 10 Festivals

1 Doors Open
Toronto's most interesting and unusual buildings open the doors to the public. 🕙 *May*

2 Pride Week
A celebration of queer culture culminating with an outlandish parade that takes over the streets. 🕙 *late Jun*

3 Beaches International Jazz Festival
The sounds of jazz, blues, and zydeco fill the air at this free streetfest as dozens of bands vie for attention. 🕙 *late Jul*

4 International Festival of Authors
Top international writers join Canada's best for readings and interviews. 🕙 *late Oct*

5 Toronto International Film Festival
Screenings and parties till you drop at North America's premier film event. 🕙 *early Sep*

6 Black History Month
Art exhibits, award ceremonies, and films to celebrate and educate. 🕙 *Feb*

7 Artsweek
A window on presenters' regular seasons of dance, theatre, film, and visual arts. 🕙 *late Sep*

8 Toronto Fringe Theatre Festival
Some of the most experimental theater in the city. 🕙 *early Jul*

9 Fringe Festival of Independent Dance Artists
Vanguard performances run the gamut from flamenco and *buthoh* to modern contact. 🕙 *mid-Aug*

10 Santé: Bloor-Yorkville Wine Festival
Celebrity winemakers and the city's best chefs join forces to offer tastings, food pairings, and seminars. 🕙 *mid-May*

7 Toronto WinterCity Festival
This festival fills two mid-winter weeks with lots of reasons to head outdoors, among them kids' events, circus performances, concerts, and fireworks. Many top attractions and restaurants offer special discounts. 🕙 *late Jan–Feb*

8 Sprockets Toronto
The best in contemporary and classic children's film is presented in this satellite of the Toronto International Film Festival. Features and shorts are geared to ages 3 to 18. Workshops offer kids a behind-the-scene glimpse of moviemaking. 🕙 *mid-Apr*

9 Toronto Festival of Storytelling
All ages are invited to listen as storytellers weave tales at venues around the city. This multicultural celebration of the oral tradition includes free and ticketed events, workshops, and films. 🕙 *late Mar*

10 Toronto International Dragon Boat Race Festival
Teams from around the world compete in a race at Centre Island – the climax of the two-day Dragon Boat festival, the largest outside Asia. Performances, crafts, and food too. 🕙 *late Jun*

For details on Toronto International Film Festival, call 416 968 3456 or visit the box office in the ManuLife Centre, main floor **See p77**

Left **Royal Ontario Museum** Right **Ontario Science Centre**

🔟 Children's Attractions

1 Royal Ontario Museum
A truly magical place for children, Canada's largest museum makes a special effort to have plenty of hands-on exhibits. The much-loved Dinosaur Gallery and mummy cases are strictly "don't touch," but the Hands-On Biodiversity Gallery enchants and educates youngsters with interactive exhibits *(see pp8–11).*

2 Hockey Hall of Fame
Budding hockey stars can test their skill whacking pucks and guarding goal at this shrine to the sport, which houses more hockey memorabilia than you can shake a stick at *(see pp26–7).*

Hockey Hall of Fame logo

3 Ontario Place
This summertime waterfront amusement park is full of fun activities for kids: waterslides, pedal boats, and the inventive Go Zone playground, to name just a few *(see pp22–3).*

4 Toronto Zoo
Exhibiting animals in their natural habitats is the policy of this zoo, which aims for meaningful education over theme-park spectacle. Seven geographic areas are represented in pavilions filled with over 450 species; large outdoor enclosures allow animals to roam freely *(see p91).*

5 Ontario Science Centre
No need to reign in the kids at this science-based learning playground. Instead, let them charge through the more than 800 hands-on exhibits encompassing everything from sports to medicine, computers to electricity *(see p91).*

6 Riverdale Farm
This agricultural education center and working farm in the middle of the city is home to many barnyard favorites – pigs, goats, sheep, horses, and chickens. Post-and-beam barns date from the 19th century. Kids are allowed to pet most of the animals and help at feeding time. ⌖ *201 Winchester St • Map E3 • Open 9am–5pm daily*

Toronto Zoo

 Share your travel recommendations on traveldk.com

SkyRider, Canada's Wonderland

Canada's Wonderland

7 This amusement park north of the city has 400 attractions, including 50 rides, a water park, and live shows. Thrill rides for older kids, tamer rides for little ones. 🖎 *9580 Jane St, Vaughan • Map A1 • Open May–Oct; hrs vary, call 905 832 8131 • Adm • www.canadas-wonderland.com*

Harbourfront

8 The kid-friendly attractions and events at this lakefront center ensure it's always busy. Kids especially love watching artisans at work in York Quay Centre's Craft Studio, the ice-skating rink *(see p42)*, and open-air concerts.

Lorraine Kimsa Theatre for Young People

9 This theater presents excellent productions that are always a hit with children. The façade of the original building, built in 1881 as a stable for streetcar-pulling horses, can still be seen. 🖎 *165 Front St E • Map M4 • 416 862 2222*

Centre Island

10 A highlight of this Toronto island is Centreville, a bustling amusement park. Some 30 old-fashioned rides include "swan" paddle boats, an 1898 carousel, and pony rides *(see p15)*.

Top 10 Places to Eat with Kids

1 Lick's
Excellent burgers and fries; 25 flavors of ice cream. 🖎 *1960 Queen St E • Map B2 • 416 691 2305*

2 Wayne Gretzky's
Pub fare, a kids' menu, and, of course, a hockey memorabilia decor. 🖎 *99 Blue Jays Way • Map J4 • 416 979 7825*

3 Five Doors North
Classic Italian pastas and grilled meats; desserts come in heroic portions. 🖎 *2088 Yonge St • Map B2 • 2416 480 6234*

4 Shopsy's
Its hot dogs are legendary, as are its smoked-meat sandwiches. 🖎 *33 Yonge St • Map L5 • 416 365 3333*

5 Grano
Upscale but kid-friendly restaurant with fantastic Italian food. 🖎 *2035 Yonge St • Map B2 • 416 440 1986*

6 Millie's Bistro
Kids' menu features pizza and grilled-cheese sandwiches. 🖎 *1980 Avenue Rd • Map B1 • 416 481 1247*

7 Mr. Greenjeans
Burgers and hot dogs for the kids, served with fun and flair. 🖎 *Eaton Centre • Map L3 • 416 979 1212*

8 MoMo's
Friendly local hang-out with Middle Eastern and vegetarian dishes. 🖎 *196 Robert St • Map H1 • 416 966 6671*

9 Le Select
Authentic French bistro fare with a wonderful kids' menu. 🖎 *432 Wellington St W • Map H4 • 416 596 6405*

10 Old Spaghetti Factory
A perennial favorite, great for groups. 🖎 *54 The Esplanade • Map L5 • 416 864 9761*

Toronto's Top 10

Vaughan, home to Canada's Wonderland, is about 20 miles (32 km) north of Toronto

Left **Church Street** Right **AIDS Memorial, Cawthra Park**

🔟 Gay & Lesbian Hangouts

1 Church Street
The intersection of Church and Wellesley Streets, the epicenter of Toronto's gay village, has been home to a large gay and lesbian community for decades. A profusion of excellent bars, restaurants, and specialty shops make the strip a great place to just hang out and soak up the scene as leathermen, muscle boys, and drag queens strut their stuff. The 519 Community Centre at 519 Church Street hosts regular social events and neighborhood gatherings, as well as offering a multitude of drop-in programs and short-term counseling. ✎ Map L1

2 Fuzion
The beautiful, relaxing courtyard, with its mini fish pond and waterfall, along with the cozy private dining rooms, make this restaurant a favorite spot during summer as well as winter. Eclectic fusion cuisine sets the standard in the village. Mixes of soulful house and lounge beats form the backdrop sound, along with occasional guest DJs. The entire dining area drifts into club/lounge mode in the late hours. ✎ 580 Church St • Map L1 • 416 800 1322

3 Cawthra Park
This popular meeting place, with its benches and greenery, is home to a permanent AIDS memorial, installed in 1993. The pillars are inscribed, upon request and with no geographic restrictions, with the names of people lost to the disease. The Universal Remembrance Plaque, added in 1995, is a tribute to those who remain unnamed. ✎ South of 519 Church St • Map L1

Buddies

4 Slack's
A fun, boisterous restaurant and lounge popular with the gals, especially on weekends, though straights are always given a warm welcome too. DJs on Friday (retro and funk) and Saturday (retro and dance) nights, when martinis flow, then the crowds are back again for brunch. ✎ 562 Church St • Map L1 • 416 928 2151

5 Glad Day Bookshop
Established in 1970 as Canada's first gay and lesbian bookstore, its excellent collection includes a wide selection of academic, fiction, and hard-to-find titles, as well as racy picture

Glad Day Bookshop

Annual Pride Week events (June) include performances, a Dyke March, and the Pride Parade; visit www.pridetoronto.com for details books and magazines. The used books section on the second floor is definitely worth checking out. 🔊 598A Yonge St • Map L1 • 416 961 4162, 1 877 783 3725

Woody's
A stuffed rhinoceros head presiding over the bar greets patrons at this local favorite. A pool table and continuously running soft-core videos keep the clientele entertained, as do special events, like the popular Best Chest contest, here and at sibling bar Sailor, next door. 🔊 467 Church St • Map L1 • 416 972 0887

Byzantium
Designed to the hilt with a long martini bar and featuring spinning DJs for after-dinner dancing on the weekends, this stylish restaurant draws gays and straights alike. The intimate dining area is separated from the bar by moving panels. The food is great too, especially the *moules frites*. 🔊 499 Church St • Map L1 • 416 922 3859

Buddies in Bad Times Theatre
This groundbreaking theater company, established in 1979, is the city's oldest and largest venue for queer-culture productions. Renowned for innovative, edgy works, productions often push the boundaries of artistic convention and sometimes even propriety – but that's precisely the point. Special events include Hysteria, a multidisciplinary festival celebrating women (bra art is just one highlight). 🔊 12 Alexander St • Map L1 • 416 975 8555

Tallulah's Cabaret
Things get down and dirty with drag shows, burlesque, and much more at this performance

Woody's and Sailor

space cum nightclub that caters to the weekend party crowd. On Friday nights, alternative rock warms up the dance floor, while Saturdays get going with danceable pop. The cabaret is located in the Buddies in Bad Times Theatre building. 🔊 12 Alexander St • Map L1 • 416 975 8555

Hanlan's Point Beach
This secluded Toronto Island beach has the city's only official clothing-optional area. (Don't take off your clothes until you reach the well-signed, fenced section at the south end.) In 1999, the Point reclaimed its status as a nude beach, as it had been between 1894 and 1930, enabling nudists and cruisers alike to once again soak up the sun in the buff. "No swimming" warnings are posted when water pollution levels are high (see p15). 🔊 Map B6

Left **Colborne Lane** Right **Canoe**

🔟 Restaurants

1 Colborne Lane

This modern, post-industrial restaurant is a mecca for lovers of molecular gastronomy, and Claudio Aprile is Toronto's most proficient and enigmatic culinary maestro. His tasting menu, bursting with delicious surprises, is a must. Both *Food & Wine Magazine* and *Condé Nast Traveler* voted Colborne Lane as one of the most exciting new restaurants in the world. ◈ 45 Colborne St • Map K4 • 416 368 9009 • $$$$

2 The Fifth

This restaurant styles itself as a club (and yes, non-members do pay slightly more); the freight-elevator ride to the fifth floor loft only adds to the exclusive feel of the place. A *prix fixe* menu favors French classics such as *foie gras*, duck breast, and langoustine. In winter, candles, fireplace, and couches make things lavishly cozy. In summer, try for a table on the rooftop terrace. ◈ 225 Richmond St W • Map J4 • 416 979 3005 • $$$$$

3 Canoe

Stellar views from the 54th floor of the Toronto Dominion Bank Tower make this one of the most enchanting rooms in the city. Lunchtime business crowds may close deals over lobster clubhouse sandwiches on brioche, but the evening ambience is decidedly more romantic. Menu mainstays include quintessentially Canadian caribou and bison *(see p69)*.

Starfish's catch of the day

4 Starfish

This low-key, sophisticated restaurant specializes in fish and seafood, particularly oysters – almost 20 varieties of them, with fresh French oysters on Thursdays. Preparations such as lobster bisque give a nod to Gallic cooking, with its classically complex flavors. Save room for dessert, all of which are excellent. The reasonably priced wine list is mainly French *(see p89)*.

5 Senses

Presentation is at its artful best at this exquisite restaurant, where beauty matches flavor to titillate all the senses. Chef Claudio Aprile's tasting menu mixes Asian, Latin, and French elements to delightful effect, with many vegetarian-friendly choices. Scrumptious desserts. ◈ 328 Wellington St W • Map J4 • 416 935 0400 $$$$

Senses

For restaurant price ranges **See p69**

Chiado

Lai Wah Heen
With exceptional Cantonese cuisine, this elegant two-level restaurant in the Metropolitan Hotel redefines and updates classic Chinese fare. Haute details include silver chopstick rests and starched linens on the round tables, which are suitable for large groups and conducive to sharing (smaller tables also available). Sunday *dim sum* is particularly popular. ⊗ *108 Chestnut St • Map K3 • 416 977 9899 • $$$$*

Chiado
Dine on the freshest fish and seafood to be had in the city, flown in from the world's wharfs daily and transformed into the most luxurious of Portuguese fare. The wine list is replete with unusual offerings which the waitstaff are expert at elucidating and pairing with dishes. Try wines by the glass at the tapas-style wine bar, Senhor Antonio, in the restaurant's cozy annex addition, where cheaper prices mean some of the best value in town. ⊗ *864 College St • Map A3 • 416 538 1910 • $$$$$*

Sushi Kaji
Masterful chef Mitsuhiro Kaji creates the city's premiere Japanese cuisine at this farwestend restaurant. There are two private rooms, but better to perch at the eight-seat sushi bar to enjoy the food-as-theater experience. Premium sakes are the perfect accompaniment to excellent – and generously portioned – sushi, *sashimi*, and creative cooked offerings *(see p95)*.

Noce
This intimate restaurant serves marvelous Italian food, delivered with welcoming, friendly service. The homemade pasta specials are always superb, as are grilled and roasted meats. The summer patio is great for al fresco dining. ⊗ *075 Queen St W • Map B4 • 416 504 3463 • $$$$*

Ultra Supper Club
This elegantly appointed eatery strikes a fashionable balance between restaurant and nightclub. Chef Chris Zielinski's ambitious menu places emphasis on seasonality and originality. Enjoy a cocktail on the rooftop terrace in summer. ⊗ *314 Queen St W • Map C4 • 416 263 0330 • $$$$$*

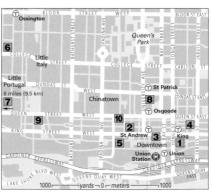

Toronto's Top 10

Left **Verveine** Right **Lakeview Lunch**

Brunches

Verveine
The decor is soothing (soft lighting and linens), the food high-end comfort: smoked salmon with truffled scrambled eggs, poached eggs on croissant *(see p89)*. ◈ $$

Lakeview Lunch
Slide into a booth – part of the old-style diner decor – and choose from a menu that focuses on eggs and burger classics. Good milkshakes. ◈ *1132 Dundas St W • Map A4 • 416 535 2828 • $*

Courtyard Café
This elegant restaurant in the venerable Windsor Arms Hotel has for decades been a city favorite for a romantic Sunday brunch. The traditional-style buffet includes salmon, made-to-order omelets, roasts, and desserts. ◈ *18 St Thomas St • Map C3 • 416 921 2921 • $$$$*

Courtyard Café

Bonjour Brioche
This bakery cum café is popular with locals, so arrive early to get a seat. Brioches and croissants (in several flavors) are baked on the premises and melt-in-your-mouth fresh. Sandwiches on chewy baguettes are excellent. ◈ *812 Queen St E • Map F4 • 416 406 1250 • $*

Fruit tart, Bonjour Brioche

Gallery Grill
The neo-Gothic splendor of the University of Toronto's Hart House *(see p76)* sets the tone of refined tradition, and the menu adds sparkle to the sedate surroundings. Fine sandwiches, soups, and an extensive selection of wines by the glass. ◈ *7 Hart House Circle • Map J1 • 416 978 2445 • Closed Sat • $$*

Pink Pearl
The Chinese tradition of selecting *dim sum* items such as shrimp and pork dumplings, stuffed noodles, sticky rice, and barbecue pork buns from passing carts turns brunch into a festive occasion at this Yorkville restaurant. ◈ *120 Avenue Rd • Map C2 • 416 966 3631 • $$*

Dooney's
This Annex institution hops on the weekends, when locals line up for tasty omelets, blueberry pancakes, "samnscram" – scrambled eggs with smoked

salmon and scallions – and strong lattes. Some patrons, local writers among them, hold down tables for hours, immersed in the neighborly atmosphere. ® *511 Bloor St W • Map B3 • 416 536 3293 • $*

Xacutti
Cardamom scented butter milk biscuits and Bombay scrambled eggs spice up brunch at this Little Italy standby. Cool your tastebuds with a free shooter of the daily smoothie. The weekend brunch menu is also great, though it veers away from Indian food. Reservations are recommended for dinner. ® *503 College St • Map B3 • 416 393 3957 • $$$*

Aunties and Uncles
A charmingly eclectic place. Arrive early, before the crowds scoop up all the Belgian waffles. Soups, salads, omelets, and sandwiches are excellent, the juice freshly squeezed. ® *74 Lippincott St • Map B3 • 416 324 1375 • $*

Counter seating at Swan

Swan
A Formica-topped counter and reclaimed diner booths lend this bustling spot a 1950s feel, but the food is decidedly contemporary. Eggs are scrambled with smoked oysters and pancetta, sautéed spinach accompanies trout eggs benny. Excellent Americano coffee, but alas, no free refills. ® *892 Queen St W • Map B4 • 416 532 0452 • $$*

Top 10 Best Snacks

1 Chinese Buns
Steamed dough filled with savory meat, vegetables, or sweet coconut and red bean paste. Eat piping hot.

2 Souvlaki
Grilled chunks of marinated lamb, beef, pork, or chicken smothered in garlicky Greek *tzaziki* sauce and often wrapped in pita bread.

3 Falafel
Deep-fried chickpea balls in pita pockets stuffed with *tahini* sauce, onion, and tomato – a Lebanese specialty.

4 Bubble Tea
An Asian concoction of sweet, flavored cold tea, milk, and tapioca pearls.

5 Gelato
More refreshing and lighter than ice cream, Italian ices come in an assortment of flavors, from lemon to caramel.

6 Corn on the Cob
Little India street vendors prepare grilled corn glazed with lemon juice and spices.

7 Hot Dogs
Ubiquitous outdoor carts grill hot dogs, veggie dogs, and sausages. Polish sausage is a favorite, piled high with all the fixings – pickles, sauerkraut, and hot mustard.

8 Jamaican Roti
Soft flat bread encase a variety of fillings, from curried goat or chicken to spinach and squash. Hot sauce is optional.

9 Churrasco Chicken
Spiked with tangy Portuguese *piri piri* sauce, then barbecued to perfection; served on a bun or with roasted spuds.

10 Roasted Chestnuts
Sidewalk vendors sell steaming-hot smoky-flavored chestnuts in summer and fall.

Toronto's Top 10

 Brunch is often served on weekends only; phone ahead to confirm

Left **Avenue** Right **The Roof Lounge**

🔟 Bars & Clubs

1 Crush
Just as diners are ordering dessert, the lights are dimmed and the music turned up, officially ushering in the night to this restaurant and wine bar. A terrific selection of wines, many by the glass and fairly priced. The splendid loft space has a large adjoining patio (see p67).

2 The Roof Lounge
A haunt of creative types, this bar atop the Park Hyatt Hotel offers refuge from daily stresses. In winter, a fireplace and huge leather chairs beckon; in summer, spectacular views from the terrace (see p80).

Cameron House ant sculpture

3 Guvernment
Rave gear isn't mandatory for joining the 3,000 clubbers who, animated by lasers pulsing to the house, progressive, and trance beating from a deafening sound system, party into the wee hours. Five lounges offer a brief respite from the cavernous split-level dance floor. Concerts are held at adjoining Kool Haus (see p67).

4 Avenue
It's all about style at this busy see-and-be-seen bar on the ground floor of the prestigious Four Seasons Hotel in fashionable Yorkville. At your table, adept servers prepare the perfect cocktail in a miniature shaker; nary a drop is spilled. At the bar, business tycoons talk takeovers while scoping out the room (see p80).

5 Cameron House
Giant "ants" on the front of this former flophouse signal a different bar experience. Unspoiled by the acts that played here before making it big, this low-key bar is dedicated to up-and-coming musicians. Join foot-stomping regulars on weekend evenings for pay-what-you-can country music (see p80).

6 Circa
Nightlife luminary Peter Gatien's 55,000-sq-ft (5,200-sq-m) facility hosts art, music, and fashion events during the week. World class DJs and artists liven up the weekends (see p67).

Guvernment

Recommend your favorite bar on traveldk.com

Irish Embassy Pub & Grill

Top Ten Places to See Live Music

Opera House
An eclectic range of bands plays beneath the ornate proscenium arch. All-ages shows and blues nights pack the place. 🕲 735 Queen St E • Map F4

Rivoli
Booking top alternative rock bands has made this spot a Toronto landmark. 🕲 334 Queen St W • Map H4

El Mocambo
Revived by a recent facelift, this national landmark presents rock, folk, funk, and more on its two floors. 🕲 464 Spadina Ave • Map H2

Horseshoe Tavern
The Rolling Stones kicked off their 1997 world tour at this venerable watering hole. 🕲 370 Queen St W • Map H4

The Trane Studio
Jazz and all its manifestations in African, Latin, and world music styles are celebrated here. 🕲 964 Bathurst St

The Rex Hotel
The hotel's jazz and blues bar attracts Canada's finest musicians. 🕲 194 Queen St W • Map J3

Hugh's Room
Enjoy popular folk musicians in an intimate space. 🕲 2261 Dundas St W • Map A2

Lee's Palace
This gritty joint hosts edgy rock bands. 🕲 529 Bloor St W • Map B3

Reservoir Lounge
Jazz, boogie-woogie, and jump blues; southern cuisine. 🕲 52 Wellington St E • Map L4 • Closed Sun

Phoenix
Rock bands, and dancing on DJ'd theme nights. 🕲 410 Sherbourne St • Map M1

Irish Embassy Pub & Grill
Pub lovers will feel at home with the mahogany bar and stool and booth seating set among the marble columns of this historic bank building. Good choice of beers on tap, and tasty pub food, including bison burgers. 🕲 49 Yonge St • Map L4 • 416 866 8282

Easy & The Fifth
The high-ceilinged dance club of this restaurant/bar venue (see p52) caters to the 25-plus crowd. Bouncers ignore the jeans-clad in favor of those casual-smart; once inside, grab a drink at the long bar, then dance to R&B and top-40 music or play pool under the watchful gaze of cigar smokers in the sideroom (see p67).

Lula Lounge
Lively bands and hot DJs play everything Latin, from salsa to merengue. Enjoy dinner before the show, arrive later for drinks, or go all out with a dance lesson-dinner-show package (see p80).

Bar at Canoe
On the 54th floor of the TD Bank Tower (see p64), this sophisticated spot caters to corporate wheelers and dealers (reduced to size against the magnificent view of Lake Ontario), as well as locals and visitors out for a special night. Excellent wines, cocktails, and beer selection (see p67).

Most live music venues are licensed bars and entrance is limited to those 19 years and older, unless an event is specifically all-ages

57

Left **Street sign, West Queen West Art and Design** Right **Fresh fish, Chinatown**

Shopping Destinations

1 West Queen West Art & Design District
As artists move farther west on Queen Street to more affordable quarters between Bathurst Street and Gladstone Avenue, so too do the independent and experimental art galleries and the clothing shops showcasing funky Canadian designers. The abundance of antique and used furniture, trendy kitchenware, and offbeat and vintage clothing shops guarantees interesting finds *(see p76)*.

2 Queen Street West
Artists after cheap rent settled among the textile shops along Queen Street between University Avenue and Bathurst Street in the early 1980s. Galleries and shops bursting with art, hip clothing, handcrafted jewelry, and home-decor items followed. These days, chains such as Montreal-based Le Chateau, The Gap, and Banana Republic have a definite presence as well. ✪ *Map G4–J4*

Shop window, Queen Street East

3 Kensington Market
This chaotic enclave is a true gem. Once a Jewish market, the predominant ethnic flavor is now Portuguese and West Indian, with strong hints of Asian and Hispanic. The many food shops reflect this, stocked as they are with cassava, cornbread, pulses, cheese, salted cod, and spices. Fruit and veggies are some of the freshest – and cheapest – in the city. The waft of incense and strains of Reggae will lead you to the dimly lit secondhand clothing stores, many with a goth or hippie flair, nestled in Victorian houses *(see p73)*.

Antique Centre

4 Toronto Antique Centre
This market brings over 20 dealers together under one roof – an antique-lover's dream. Georgian silver, majolica, vintage luggage, militaria, prints and maps, and furniture are just some of the treasures awaiting you. ✪ *276 King St W • Map J4 • 416 345 9941*

5 Queen Street East
Lovers of vintage clothes, radios and vinyl, and furniture from the 1960s and 1970s – some from well-known designers – will have a shopping fest along this eclectic stretch. Perhaps inspired by their trendy retro design neighbors, modern home-decor shops and interior design firms are also making this area home *(see p39)*.

Shop window, Yorkville

Yorkville
Clustered in this upscale district, choice boutiques and fine art galleries offer everything the well-heeled and -monied traveler desires. Even the local mall, Hazelton Lanes, harbors luxury shops such as a Rolls Royce dealership and Whole Foods Market, which tempts with mouth-watering but pricey prepared foods to fill the picnic basket (see p77).

Chinatown
You may think you're in Hong Kong as you browse along Spadina Avenue and Dundas Street, speculating on the use of exotic ingredients such as dried shrimp and the odoriferous durian fruit, or eyeing the dizzying array of Chinese housewares, knickknacks, and herbal medicines on offer. A terrific place to find unusual souvenirs at low prices (see p73).

Toronto Eaton Centre
Anchored on each end by a major department store – The Bay and Sears – this shopping oasis has something for every taste and bank balance. Books, plasma TVs, gourmet cookware, fashion – the range of goods across hundreds of stores is huge (see pp24–5).

St. Lawrence Market
Considered by gastronomes around the globe as one of the world's best markets, a visit here is reason enough for food lovers to travel to Toronto. A huge selection of meat, fish, cheese, and produce, as well as hand-crafted gifts, make for a one-of-a-kind experience. Vendors pushing food samples and buskers add to the dynamic atmosphere; frequent special events and festivals liven things up even more. When you can't carry another thing, visit the free parcel check on the west side of the lower level, outside (see p86).

Bloor Street
Bloor Street between Church Street and Avenue Road is lined with international designer boutiques: Gucci, Tiffany's, Hermès, Chanel, and Max Mara, as well as excellent homegrown stores. Drop by fine jewelers Birks; William Ashley China, a top-notch china and glass store; Holt Renfrew, a small department store specializing in high-end clothing; Harry Rosen, a superb men's clothing store with impeccable service; and the Roots flagship store, offering quality leather and sportswear (see p77).

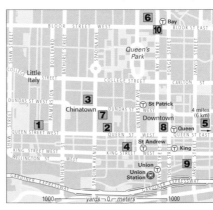

AROUND
TOWN

TORONTO'S TOP 10

Left **Marina at Harbourfront** Right **Photo Passage, York Quay Centre**

Harbourfront & the Financial District

THE STREETS OF HARBOURFRONT *and the Financial District combine old and new in a vibrant mix. Along the shores of Lake Ontario, the origins of the city can be traced to the establishment of Fort York in 1793. As the town of York grew, spreading north from the lake, financial institutions settled around Bay and King streets. Today, modern skyscrapers, interspersed with historic buildings, dot the district, and historic vaudeville theaters, restored to their original splendor, anchor an exuberant entertainment scene.*

🔟 Sights

1. Toronto Islands
2. Queen's Quay Terminal
3. York Quay Centre
4. Rogers Centre
5. Toronto-Dominion Centre
6. CN Tower
7. Fort York
8. Hockey Hall of Fame
9. Ontario Place
10. Toronto Music Garden

Detail from *The Audience*, by Michael Snow, Rogers Centre

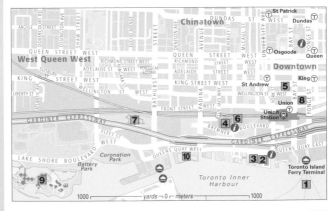

Queen's Quay Terminal

York Quay Centre

This converted warehouse is the center for a diverse range of recreational and cultural activities, from exhibitions to performances to skating. Visitors can watch artisans create glass and clay pieces at the craft studio, check out the four galleries, and browse in the excellent shop selling hand-crafted gifts. The Photo Passage exhibits contemporary Canadian photographic works; other venues regularly program author readings and theater performances. A café overlooking the pond, which becomes a popular skating rink in winter (see p42), serves light meals and snacks. ✆ 235 Queens Quay W • Map K6 • 416 973 4000 • Open 10am–9pm Tue–Sat

Toronto Islands

Recreational opportunities – from sunbathing to cycling to children's amusement rides – abound on the car-free islands, Toronto's summer playground for more than a century. Ferries depart regularly for the islands from the foot of Bay Street; the 10-minute trip across the harbor offers unparalleled views of downtown (see pp14–15).

Queen's Quay Terminal

In a grand 1926 building that looks like a layered cake, this retail complex is bursting with bou-tiques selling unusual gift items, Native art, crafts, clothing, kitchen-ware, toys, and chocolates. Many restaurants, several with patios overlooking the water, offer good fare. Harbor cruises depart along-side the terminal. ✆ 207 Queens Quay W • Map K6 • 416 203 0510 • Open 10am–6pm daily

Rogers Centre

At the base of the CN Tower, this sports and large-events venue is home to the city's baseball team, the Blue Jays, and football team, the Argonauts. When built in 1989, it had the world's only fully retractable roof of its kind, which takes just 20 minutes to open or close. When teams are not in action, you can tour the facility and peek into players' dressing rooms. Outside, on the northeast corner of the building, a frieze by Toronto artist Michael Snow depicts 14 spectators. ✆ 1 Blue Jays Way • Map J5 • 416 341 1707

Harbourfront

 For information about upcoming sports events and concerts at the Rogers Centre, visit www.rogerscentre.com

Toronto-Dominion Centre

This six-tower complex is one of the most important pieces of architecture in the city *(see p36)*. The black steel I-beams of the 1968 Toronto Dominion Bank Tower are trademark Mies van der Rohe (1886–1969), and perfectly reflect the architect's modernist dictum that "Less is more." In the plaza, a circular bronze sculpture, Al McWilliams's *Wall and Chairs*, echoes the towers' austerity. Below ground is a shopping mall, the only one van der Rohe ever designed. ◎ 55 King St W • Map K4

CN Tower

Soaring 1,815 ft (553 m) above downtown Toronto, this is the defining icon of the city's skyline and

Toronto-Dominion Centre

the world's tallest free-standing structure. On the mezzanine level, check out the exhibit on the tower's construction before "bungee jumping" from the top at an interactive daredevil display. Then let a glass-fronted elevator zip you, in less than a minute, to one of four lookout levels. The

Canada's War Against the US

On June 18, 1812, the US declared war on Great Britain and, for months, battled at various border outposts such as Detroit and Queenston Heights. In April 1813, American troops invaded York (as Toronto was then called), occupying the town, burning the Parliament buildings, and destroying much of Fort York. Although the US won the Battle of York, they soon abandoned the town to fight battles in the Niagara Peninsula, with mixed results. The American war with Britain ended in stalemate on December 24, 1814, with the signing of the Treaty of Ghent.

extra fee for the highest lookout, Sky Pod, ensures fewer crowds. The revolving restaurant, 360, offers fine food in serene surroundings *(see pp12–13)*.

Fort York

This garrison, established by Lieutenant Governor John Graves Simcoe in 1793 to protect the growing city, is the site of the fierce Battle of York during the War of 1812, when the US invaded Upper Canada. Home to the country's largest collection of War of 1812 buildings (brick structures that replaced the fort's original wood cabins), the restored fort has fascinating displays of historic military artifacts. Guides in costume lead tours and give period music, musket, and drill demonstrations. ◎ 100 Garrison Rd • Map G5 • Open Jan–May: 10am–4pm Mon–Fri, 10am–5pm Sat–Sun; Victoria Day–Labour Day: 10am–5pm daily • Adm

Hockey Hall of Fame

Hockey fans will be fascinated by the memorabilia on view at this museum dedicated to Canada's favorite sport. Everything from masks personalized by goalies to hand-carved skates from the 1840s reflect the history of the game. Have your photo taken with the iconic Stanley Cup, then test your skill at the game at the interactive exhibits *(see pp26–7)*.

Ontario Place

This family-oriented, summertime amusement park built beside, around, and literally on top of Lake Ontario embraces its

Cinesphere, Ontario Place

waterfront perch with enthusiasm. Water-fun options include giant waterslides and river rides. Visitors looking for more serene activities can paddle around the lagoon in a pedal boat. The Cinesphere IMAX theater, housed in a futuristic Triodetic dome, shows documentary films on subjects ranging from caves to rainforests to auto racing on its six-story screen *(see pp22–3)*. ✆ 955 Lakeshore Blvd W • Map A5–A6 • Open Victoria Day–Labour Day: 10:30am–8pm daily • Adm

Toronto Music Garden

This playfully elegant garden, a collaboration between famed cellist Yo Yo Ma, landscape architect Julie Moir Messervy, and Toronto landscape architects, was inspired by J. S. Bach's *First Suite for Unaccompanied Cello*. Each dance movement in the suite – allemande, courante, sarabande, menuett, and gigue – plus a prelude, is represented by the plantings in one of the six sections of the garden. Summer concerts are held in the grassy amphitheater. ✆ 475 Queens Quay W • Map H6

Toronto Music Garden

An Art Walk

Morning

🕐 Start at **Commerce Court North** *(see p66)* to admire the stunning lobby. Walk west to Bay St and the **TD Centre**, noting the **Wall and Chairs** sculpture in the plaza *(see p37)* and Joe Fafard's life-sized **bronze cows** lounging on the lawn behind 77 King St W.

Just around the corner at 234 Bay St is the **Design Exchange** *(see p66)*. Explore it for an hour before enjoying a pan-Asian lunch at **Kubo DX**, on the first floor.

Afternoon

Zigzag your way to Simcoe Park, on Front St west of Wellington, and the luminous **Anish Kapoor sculpture**. A monument beside it honors city founders. Continue west along Front, past the CBC at No. 250, noting the **Glenn Gould sculpture**, in memory of the eccentric pianist. You'll soon come to Sky-Dome, and **The Audience**, Michael Snow's larger-than-life fans *(see p37)*.

Turn left on Spadina Ave; crossing the bridge, look to your left to see **Eldon Garnet's memorial** commemorating Chinese laborers who helped build Canada's railroad. It's five minutes to the lake, and just west on Queens Quay, **Toronto Music Garden**, in bloom spring to fall. Wander this oasis for an hour, then walk 15 minutes east to **York Quay Centre** to watch artisans at work and stroll the **Photo Passage** *(see p63)*.

End the day with a steak dinner at **Harbour Sixty** (60 Harbour St), in the opulent former Harbour Commission building.

Around Town – Harbourfront & the Financial District

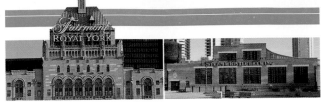

Left **Fairmont Royal York** Right **Steam Whistle Brewing**

🔟 Best of the Rest

Union Station
Built by 1921 but not opened until 1927 due to legalities, this elegant train station features a frieze citing Canadian destinations *(see p37)*. ◈ 65 Front St W • Map K5

401 Richmond Street
Many of the city's best artist-run galleries are here in this gorgeous old warehouse. Exhibit openings are often held Thursday evenings and Saturday afternoons. ◈ 401 Richmond St W • Map H4

Design Exchange
This gallery showcases innovative Canadian postwar design *(see p34)*. ◈ 234 Bay St • Map K4 • open 10am–6pm Mon–Fri, noon–5pm Sat–Sun • Adm to special exhibits

Toronto Dominion Gallery of Inuit Art
An outstanding collection of postwar Inuit sculpture *(see p35)*. ◈ 79 Wellington St W • Map K4 • Open 8am–6pm Mon–Fri, 10am–4pm Sat–Sun

Steam Whistle Brewing
This railroad roundhouse now functions as a microbrewery. Tour the facilities, then sample the tasty results at the bar. ◈ 255 Bremner Blvd • Map J5 • Open May–Aug: noon–6pm daily; Sep–Apr: noon–6pm Mon–Sat

Commerce Court North
The star of Toronto's early skyscrapers, this massive 34-story Romanesque structure housing the Canadian Imperial Bank of Commerce was the tallest building in Canada when completed in 1931. Today it matches aesthetically, if not in height, its towering neighbors. ◈ 25 King St W • Map L4

Fairmont Royal York
This grand château-style hotel *(see p116)*, once the largest in the British Commonwealth, was built in 1928 by the Canadian Pacific Railway. ◈ 100 Front St W • Map K5

Air Canada Centre
Home to basketball's Raptors and hockey's Maple Leafs, the arena is in the old Toronto Postal Delivery Building. Carvings on the façade depict the history of communications. ◈ 40 Bay St • Map K5

Exhibition Place
Princes' Gates herald the entrance to the Canadian National Exhibition's fairgrounds, hosting major events such as the Royal Agricultural Winter Fair. ◈ Map A5

Power Plant Contemporary Art Gallery
Toronto's premiere contemporary art public gallery. ◈ 231 Queens Quay W • Map K6 • open noon–6pm Tue, Thu–Sun, noon–8pm Wed • Adm

The Air Canada Centre offers one-hour tours of the facility; call 416 815 5982 or visit www.theaircanadacentre.com for details

Left **Wheat Sheaf Tavern** Right **The Paddock**

🔟 Bars & Clubs

1 Crush
Wine is king at this hip loft-space bar/restaurant, but other, equally delicious, libations are also poured *(see p56)*. 🌐 455 King St W • Map H4 • 416 977 1234 • Closed Sun in winter

2 Bar at Canoe
It's a heady experience sipping the perfect martini while gazing at the city from the top of a skyscraper *(see p57)*. 🌐 66 Wellington St W • Map K4 • 416 364 0054 • Closed Sat–Sun

3 Easy & The Fifth
Savor the bouncer escort to the fifth-floor bar, or pass muster to enter the two-level club and dance the night away to R&B and top 40 *(see p57)*. 🌐 225 Richmond St W (enter via alley) • Map J4 • 416 979 3005 • open Thu–Sat • Adm

4 Library Bar
Tucked inside the Fairmont Royal York hotel *(see p66)*, this bar has a gentleman's-club atmosphere, with its book-lined walls and leather chairs that promote relaxation as you imbibe a noble cognac. 🌐 100 Front St W • Map K5 • 416 368 2511

5 The Paddock
Although red leather banquettes prompt a twinge of 1950s nostalgia, this bar is firmly rooted in the 21st century with an inventive cocktail menu and good selection of draft beers. 🌐 178 Bathurst St • Map G4 • 416 504 9997

6 Guvernment
Serious party-goers storm this weekends-only dance club and bar complex. Lineups move surprisingly quickly *(see p56)*. 🌐 132 Queens Quay E • Map M5 • 416 869 0045 • Adm

7 Circa
Multiple themed rooms, art events, and performances make Circa Toronto's most exciting nightclub experience. 🌐 126 John St • Map J4 • 416 979 0044 • Adm

8 Wheat Sheaf Tavern
Toronto's oldest tavern dates to about 1848. Enjoy chicken wings and a pint to TV sports or on the deck. 🌐 667 King St W • Map G4 • 416 504 9912

9 Academy of Spherical Arts
Antique billiard tables, great beer, and good food make for an unforgettable experience in this lofty, renovated billiard factory. 🌐 38 Hanna Ave • Map A5 • 416 532 2782

10 Brant House
Housed in a former factory, this is one of Toronto's most elegant and popular restaurant-lounge-dance club hybrids. 🌐 522 King St W • Map H4 • 416 703 2800

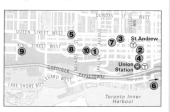

Note: Patrons of Toronto bars and clubs must be of legal drinking age – 19 years or older – unless an event is specifically all-ages

Left **Princess of Wales Theatre** Right **Elgin Theatre**

Theaters

Canon Theatre
Big musicals have replaced vaudeville on the bill. The 1920s interior is a fantasy of gilt-framed mirrors and chandeliers, a magnificent staircase and dome. *263 Yonge St • Map L3 • 416 872 1212*

Royal Alexandra Theatre
Saved from demolition, this 1906 theater has been returned to Edwardian finery. A lovely mural tops the dramatic proscenium arch. Musicals and drama. *260 King St W • Map J4 • 416 872 1212*

Princess of Wales Theatre
This venue for hit musicals opened in 1993, the first privately developed large theater the city had seen since 1907. The interior by Toronto design team Yabu Pushelberg spares no expense. Wall and ceiling murals by American minimalist Frank Stella. *300 King St W • Map J4 • 416 872 1212*

Premiere Dance Theatre
The *crème de la crème* of modern dance, by both local and visiting companies, has graced this stage. *207 Queens Quay W • Map K6 • 416 973 4000*

Elgin Theatre
The lower half of the double-decker Elgin and Winter Garden Theatre Centre was built in 1913 as a movie house and, with its lavish gilding and proscenium arch, is a historic gem. *189 Yonge St • Map L3 • 416 314 2901 (tickets), 416 314 2871 (tours)*

Winter Garden Theatre
This room high above Elgin Theatre is aptly named. On the ceiling, some 5,000 beech leaves glitter in the lantern light. *189 Yonge St • Map L3 • 416 314 2901 (tickets), 416 314 2871 (tours)*

Theatre Passe Muraille
This two-stage venue has led the way with innovative Canadian productions since the 1960s, when it launched works developed by troupes of actors. *16 Ryerson Ave • Map G3 • 416 504 7529*

Factory Theatre
One of Toronto's oldest houses shows works by Canadian playwrights. Many masters, including local George F. Walker, got their start here. *125 Bathurst St • Map G4 • 416 504 9971*

Bluma Appel Theatre
Fans of CanStage's contemporary drama fill the seats. *27 Front St E • Map L5 • 416 366 7723*

Lorraine Kimsa Theatre For Young People
This award-winning theatre produces innovative, thought-provoking plays for the young (see p49).

Tours of the Elgin and Winter Garden theaters (5pm Thu & 11am Sat, $7) include a peek at a vaudeville-era dressing room

Price Categories

Price categories include a three-course meal for one, half a bottle of wine, and all unavoidable extra charges including tax.	
$	under $30
$$	$30–$50
$$$	$50–$80
$$$$	$80–$110
$$$$$	over $110

Above **Rodney's Oyster House**

🔟 Restaurants

1 Canoe
Upscale Canadian dishes – think caribou and Arctic char – are the *pièces de résistance* from chef Anthony Walsh's kitchen. Views from his 54th-floor room are stunning. ✆ *66 Wellington St W • Map K4 • 416 364 0054 • $$$$*

2 Bymark
Some of the freshest fish in town and extravagant *foie gras* attract a well-heeled crowd. Top selection of boutique Californian wines. ✆ *66 Wellington St W • Map K4 • 416 777 1144 • $$$$$*

3 Czehoski
This Queen West eatery turns out one of the freshest menus in the city, with unique and sometimes eccentric flavor pairings. Popular with the smart, early-30s crowd. ✆ *678 Queen St W • Map B4 • 416 366 6787 • $$$$*

4 Marben
Chef Craig Alley plays with Latin, Asian, and Cajun ideas brilliantly in this chic restaurant featuring a minimalist lounge, private alcoves, and spacious dining areas. ✆ *488 Wellington St W • Map A4 • 416 979 1990 • $$$*

5 Rain
Asian ingredients are given haute treatment. The sound of trickling water from chic water-falls soothes patrons waiting in the lounge. Diners sit at booths or a communal table. ✆ *19 Mercer St • Map J4 • 416 599 7246 • $$$$*

6 Blowfish
This sleek Japanese joint excels at sushi and *sashimi*, but cooked mains such as duck are equally delicious. ✆ *668 King St W • Map G4 • 416 860 0606 • $$$*

7 Rodney's Oyster House
Two dozen types of oysters entice mollusk fans; grilled fish round out the menu. ✆ *469 King St W • Map H4 • 416 363 8105 • $$$*

8 Niagara Street Cafe
Sophisticated organic comfort food with a nod to the Mediterranean, in a neighborly atmosphere. ✆ *169 Niagara St • Map B5 • 416 703 4222 • $$*

9 Nyood
A delightful menu consisting of 20-odd tapas-style dishes includes artisanal charcuterie, Arctic char ceviche, and other locally-sourced delicacies. ✆ *1096 Queen St W • Map H4 • 416 466 1888 • $$$*

10 Jules
Authentic French bistro fare served with flair (and great *frites*). Excellent value. ✆ *147 Spadina Ave • Map H4 • 416 348 8386*

Following pages **Swan boats, Toronto Islands**

Left **City Hall** Right **Kensington Market**

Downtown

T ORONTO IS A CITY OF NEIGHBORHOODS, *each with a distinct identity, many with an ethnic flavor, making it the most multicultural of North American cities. In Chinatown, wares from energetic vendors compete with shoppers for sidewalk space, and restaurants offer everything from take-out buns to sit-down banquets. The city's multicultural mix finds its fullest expression in Kensington Market, where Jamaican patty shops rub shoulders with Portuguese fish vendors and Latin American empanada stalls. Farther west is the Italian enclave of Little Italy, centered along College Street. Along with this heady ethnic mix, the downtown core is home to the upscale shopping area Yorkville and many fine cultural institutions, such as the Royal Ontario Museum and the Art Gallery of Ontario.*

Claes Oldenburg's *Floor Burger,* **AGO**

Sights

1. Eaton Centre
2. Art Gallery of Ontario
3. Kensington Market
4. Chinatown
5. Yorkville
6. Casa Loma
7. Bata Shoe Museum
8. Campbell House
9. City Hall
10. Royal Ontario Museum

Atrium, Eaton Centre

1 Eaton Centre

While it might seem strange that a shopping center is the city's most popular tourist attraction – according to the numbers, at any rate – this retail complex is simply a popular place to shop, meet, hang out, and people-watch. (Crowds of boisterous teenagers attest to this fact.) Its massive size – more than 300 stores – ensures that you can find practically anything you would want to buy here. Numerous restaurants, fast-food counters, and specialty treat shops round out the bill *(see pp24–5)*.

2 Art Gallery of Ontario

Particularly strong in historical and contemporary Canadian works, and host to important exhibitions, this is one of the country's top art galleries *(see pp16–17)*.

3 Kensington Market

This funky neighborhood, in a small pocket west of Spadina, is the heart of multicultural Toronto – a place where vendors from almost every corner of the globe have set up shop. Spilling out into the narrow sidewalks are stores selling an array of fruits,

vegetables, and bulk dry goods, while music blasts from open doors and loudspeakers. Pedestrians jostle with cyclists and traffic moves at a snail's pace, everyone vying for their inch of street space, particularly on Saturdays when the area is at its liveliest best. Leave the car behind and wander through the streets, soaking up the atmosphere, perhaps checking out the price of live lobster at a fish vendor's or browsing through trinkets and secondhand clothes in the many eclectic stores at the south end of Kensington Avenue *(see p58)*. Map H2

4 Chinatown

A steady flow of new Chinese immigrants keeps Toronto's main Chinatown one of the most vibrant in North America. Hundreds of authentic restaurants cater to all tastes and budgets, and there are countless shops selling Oriental wares. In recent years, Spadina Avenue has expanded to include many Vietnamese shops and restaurants *(see p38)*. Map H2–H3

Chinatown

Yorkville

Yorkville

In the 1960s, it was ground zero for hippies and the youth culture; today, this neighborhood is ground zero for establishment culture and the city's most upscale shopping. Expensive shops on Cumberland St and Yorkville Ave, between Bay St and Avenue Rd, sell luxury goods such as cosmetics, jewelry, designer fashions, antiques, and leather luggage. The area's numerous restaurants and bars cater to equally refined palates and wallets. There are also more than 20 fine-art galleries in the area, exhibiting some of the country's top names. Sidewalk cafés provide stylish perches for people-watching (see p38). • Map C3–D3

Casa Loma

Styled like a medieval castle, this grand mansion is a monument to the singular tastes and vision of Sir Henry Pellatt, a prominent financier who in 1911 commissioned renowned architect E. J. Lennox to build him a home. This immense architectural undertaking was on a scale never before seen in a private Canadian residence, with plans for 98 rooms, 12 baths,

5,000 electric lights, and an elevator. Its $3.5 million cost helped bankrupt Sir Henry less than 10 years after he and his wife moved in, but its opulence remains evident in the extravagant, restored rooms and furnishings (see pp18–19).

Bata Shoe Museum

This unusual, specialized museum celebrates footwear form and function throughout the ages and around the world. The building's playful design, echoing a stylized shoebox, houses four galleries exhibiting everything from Roman sandals to Elton John's platform boots. The exhibit of Chinese bound-foot shoes is not for the squeamish. Founded by Sonia Bata, who has scoured the world for shoes of every description, the museum also holds interesting themed exhibitions (see p35). ✆ 327 Bloor St W • Map C3 • Open 10am–5pm Tue, Wed, Fri–Sat, 10am–8pm Thu, noon–5pm Sun (open Mon Jun–Aug) • Adm

Bata Shoe Museum

Natural Air Conditioning

During the hot and humid days of a Toronto summer, Lake Ontario water does double duty. An innovative new project utilizes the cold temperature of deep lake water – from intake pipes 3 miles (5 km) out from shore, and 270 ft (83 m) deep – to provide chilled energy for air conditioning Toronto's downtown high-rises and large facilities such as the Air Canada Centre (see p66). After the transfer of energy, the water is returned not to the lake but to the city's water supply system, where it serves another crucial cooling function – as drinking water.

Campbell House

Campbell House
8 The oldest remaining building from the town of York, which in 1834 became Toronto, this Georgian mansion was built in 1822 for William Campbell, an Upper Canada judge. In 1972, the 300-ton building was moved from its original location on Adelaide St to its present location, restored, and opened to the public. Guided tours are available. ✆ *160 Queen St W • Map K3 • Open Victoria Day–Thanksgiving: 9:30am–4:30pm Mon–Fri, noon–4:30pm Sat–Sun; Thanksgiving–Victoria Day: 9:30am–4:30pm Mon–Fri • Adm*

City Hall
9 When first opened in 1965, the result of an international design competition won by Finnish architect Viljo Revell, this building was highly controversial. The two curving towers caused an uproar and possibly even led to the then mayor losing an election. The building has since become a prized landmark of the city, and the central plaza, Nathan Phillips Square, an animated symbol of civic life – a place for political demonstrations, winter ice skating, a summer farmers' market, outdoor concerts, and celebrations. Inside are murals and other fabulous artworks *(see p36)*.

Royal Ontario Museum
10 Canada's premiere museum has more than six million artifacts showcasing art, archeology, science, and nature *(see pp8–11)*.

A Downtown Walk

Morning

🕐 Start the day at the **Gardiner Museum of Ceramic Art** *(see p76)*, taking 90 minutes to peruse the permanent collections and visiting exhibit. On your way out, pop into the gift shop to have a look at the unique crafts.

Head north to Bloor St and turn left, walking a half block to the iron gates of **Philosophers' Walk**, beside the ROM *(see pp8–11)*. Take this charming footpath, which follows the course of the now buried Taddle Creek, exiting at Hoskin St in the heart of the University of Toronto campus *(see p76)*. Wander south to the Late Gothic Revival **Hart House**, lunching at **Gallery Grill** *(see p54)* on food that matches the impressive surroundings.

Afternoon

After lunch, poke around the stately common rooms and library of Hart House, noting the paintings throughout. Check out Canadian art at **Justina M. Barnicke Gallery**, too.

From Hart House turn right toward **University College** and some of the most historic buildings on campus. Stop by the **Laidlaw Wing** to visit the **University of Toronto Art Centre** *(see p35)*. Just to the south, on King's College Circle, is the 1906 **Convocation Hall**, with its Ionic-column-supported dome. Peek inside if the doors are unlocked.

From here, it's only a couple of blocks' stroll south and west to Chinatown. Indulge in a feast at **Lee Garden** (331 Spadina Ave).

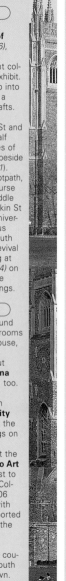

You can take a self-guided tour of City Hall between 8:30am and 4:30pm, Mon–Fri; pick up a brochure at the info counter in the lobby

75

Left **Boutique in West Queen West** Right **Graduate House, University of Toronto**

 # Best of the Rest

1 Gardiner Museum of Ceramic Art
Historic and modern pieces from around the world *(see p34)*. ◐ 111 *Queen's Park • Map C3 • 416 586 8080 (call for opening times) • Adm*

2 West Queen West
A neighborhood of eclectic shops, cutting-edge galleries, and funky cafés *(see p58)*. ◐ *Map A4–B4*

3 Bloor Street
An upscale shopping strip of high-end fashion and home-decor stores *(see p59)*. ◐ *Map C3–D3*

4 Little Italy
Bars and restaurants buzz at night; shops and delis bustle during the day *(see p38)*. ◐ *Map B3–B4*

5 Spadina Museum
An 1866 house restored with its original artifacts. Tours of the home mandatory; wandering the gardens is free. ◐ *285 Spadina Rd • Map C2 • Open Jan–Apr: noon–5pm Sat–Sun; May–Aug: noon–5pm Tue–Fri; Sep–Dec: noon–4pm Tue–Fri, noon–5pm Sat–Sun • Adm*

6 Osgoode Hall
Ontario's first law school now houses upper provincial courts. The interior of this heritage building is magnificent, the restaurant, good value. ◐ *130 Queen St W • Map K3 • 416 947 3300 • Open 9am–5pm Mon–Fri*

7 Old City Hall
Carved into the entranceway columns are caricatures of local politicians – with one exception – a straight-faced depiction of the architect. The building now serves as a courthouse *(see p36)*. ◐ *60 Queen St W • Map K3*

8 The Annex
Leafy residential sidestreets and lively cafés, ethnic restaurants, pubs, and shops along Bloor Street make for a great stroll *(see p39)*. ◐ *Map C2–C3*

9 University of Toronto
A sprawling campus of greenspaces and historic stone buildings dominates a huge swath of the central city, fanning out north, east, and west from Queen's Park up to Bloor Street. A more recent addition is the post-modern Graduate House. *(see p36)*. ◐ *Map H1–J1*

10 Ontario Legislative Building
This stately building is set in a park dotted with statues and cannons *(see p37)*. Visitors can watch politicians in action from the gallery or join in a tour of the building. ◐ *1 Queen's Park • Map K1 • Open Victoria Day–Labour Day: 8:30am–5:30pm daily; Labour Day–late May: 8:30am–4:30pm Mon–Fri*

Left **Shop window on Bloor Street** Right **Roots**

Shopping Bloor St & Yorkville

William Ashley China
Fine crystal, china, and tableware, exquisite gifts, and expert staff ensure that you won't leave without some choice purchase wrapped in elegant gold paper.
🛇 *55 Bloor St W • Map D3*

Holt Renfrew
World-class department store featuring high fashion, as well as more affordable clothing from its own label, top perfumes and cosmetics, a hair salon, epicure store, café, and free personal shopping service. 🛇 *50 Bloor St W • Map D3*

Hazelton Lanes
Shop at your leisure in this refined mall, at select fashion boutiques such as Aquascutum and TNT Blu, and in home-decor stores such as Teatro Verde. Or, for something even more special, at the Rolls Royce dealership. Then indulge in gourmet take-out from Whole Foods Market.
🛇 *55 Avenue Rd • Map C3*

Harry Rosen
Head-to-toe service is writ large at this menswear store featuring apparel from top design houses, Canali and Hugo Boss included. Suits, trousers, blazers, shirts, and all accessories, including shoes. 🛇 *82 Bloor St W • Map C3*

David's
Shoe lovers go on wild spending sprees here among the stylish footwear from hot designers.
🛇 *66 Bloor St W • Map D3*

Pusateri's
Food afficionados will love the luxury grocery items such as stuffed quail, *foie gras*, caviar, and truffle oil, and delicious prepared foods. 🛇 *57 Yorkville Ave • Map D3*

The Guild Shop
Jewelry, hand-blown glass, Inuit carvings, and more reflect the excellence of Ontario crafts.
🛇 *118 Cumberland St • Map C3*

ManuLife Centre
Movie theaters and shops such as Indigo Books, Birks jewelers, Teuscher Chocolates and Bay Bloor Radio will lure you to this mini-mall. 🛇 *55 Bloor St W • Map D3*

Thomas Hinds Tobacconists
This smoker's paradise has a walk-in humidor safeguarding a full range of Cuban and Latin American cigars, and two smoking lounges in which to enjoy them. Stellar selection of tobaccos, cigarettes, and accessories.
🛇 *8 Cumberland St • Map D3*

Roots
Quality sportswear, casual clothes, and leather goods for every member of the family.
🛇 *100 Bloor St W • Map C3*

Left **Honest Ed's** Right **Club Monaco**

🔟 Shopping Downtown

1 World's Biggest Bookstore
In a converted bowling alley just off Yonge Street, bibliophiles can browse through 12 miles (20 km) of bookshelves. Make sure you have plenty of time on your hands. ◈ *20 Edward St • Map L2*

2 Tom's Place
Be prepared to bargain for that Armani jacket – Tom will be disappointed if you don't. Men's and women's clothing from top designers at discount prices. ◈ *190 Baldwin St • Map H2*

3 The Japanese Paper Place
A huge selection of fine Japanese papers, handmade stationery, and beautiful note-books. ◈ *887 Queen St W • Map B4*

4 LCBO at Summerhill
This vast liquor store in a former train station stocks a superb selection of wines, beers, and spirits from around the world. ◈ *10 Scrivener Sq • Map D2*

5 Honest Ed's
Rock-bottom prices on a huge array of goods, from housewares to clothing, are the big draw at this garishly lit Toronto landmark. On-site optometrist, dentist, pharmacy, and TicketKing outlet too. Beware the no-return policy. ◈ *581 Bloor St W • Map B3*

6 Club Monaco
Cool and sleek characterize the clothes and accessories of this monolithic retailer, started in Toronto in 1985. The chic flagship location has the widest selection. ◈ *157 Bloor St W • Map C3*

7 Umbra
This hard-to-miss concept store for Canada's pre-eminent design showcases its casual, contemporary home-design accessories in a pink glass box building. ◈ *165 John St • Map J3*

8 Courage My Love
Inexpensive vintage clothes; beads, jewelry, and trinkets from Asia, India, and South America pack this small incense-perfumed space. ◈ *14 Kensington Ave • Map H2*

9 Comrags
Locals Joyce Gunhouse and Judy Cornish have made an international name for themselves with their swishy urban-romantic women's clothing line. ◈ *654 Queen St W • Map G3*

10 M.A.C.
Don't be scared off by the staff – male and female – decked in all black, including eyeliner. These skilled makeup artists will demystify the products in this hip, uni-sex line created for the fashion industry. ◈ *89 Bloor St W • Map C3*

It's a good idea to inquire about the shop's return policy before making a purchase

Price Categories

Price categories include a three-course meal for one, half a bottle of wine, and all unavoidable extra charges including tax.

$	under $30
$$	$30–$50
$$$	$50–$80
$$$$	$80–$110
$$$$$	over $110

Above **Opus**

🔟 Restaurants & Cafés

1 Cluck, Grunt, and Low
Cocktails in Mason jars and some of the best slow-cooked meat in the city are available here. Try the wild turkey ice cream for dessert. 🌐 *362 Bloor St W • Map C3 • 416 962 5050 • $$$*

2 Joso's
Over-the-top decor (nude busts predominate) sets the tone at this seafood emporium. Customize your platter with the day's catch. Fine pastas, risottos, and meat dishes too. 🌐 *202 Davenport Rd • Map C2 • 416 925 1903 • $$$*

3 Opus
This refined dining room has one of the best wine lists in the city. Tuna tartare with caviar, and the roasted meats get top marks. 🌐 *37 Prince Arthur Ave • Map C3 • 416 921 3105 • $$$$*

4 Splendido
Upscale Italian, with high-end indulgences such as veal and sweetbread. Excellent fish mains, and an impressive cheese plate. The service in this handsome dining room is impeccable. 🌐 *88 Harbord St • Map C3 • 416 929 7788 • $$$$*

5 Le Sélect
Classic French bistro dishes such as onion soup and *cassoulet*, and reasonable *prix fixe* meals. Diners help themselves to bread from the baskets hanging above the tables. 🌐 *432 Wellington St W • Map H4 • 416 596 6405 • $$$*

6 Queen Mother Café
Thai and Laotian flavors characterize the menu at this established spot; pictures of the Queen Mum, the decor. Opt for a cozy booth, or ask for directions to the secluded back patio. Wicked desserts. 🌐 *208 Queen St W • Map K3 • 416 598 4719 • $*

7 The Coffee Mill
This unpretentious Hungarian restaurant is a Yorkville mainstay. Tucked away in a mall, it serves goulash soup, *Wiener Schnitzel*, homemade desserts, and excellent espresso. 🌐 *99 Yorkville Ave • Map C3 • 416 920 2108 • $*

8 7 West Café
Warm and cozy, thanks to a fireplace and numerous rooms, though it can get crowded. Salads, sandwiches, pastas, and desserts are dished up 24/7. 🌐 *7 Charles St W • Map D3 • 416 928 9041 • $*

9 Bistro 990
French provincial fare is the specialty in this romantic room. The wine list and celebrity-spotting opportunities are particularly good. 🌐 *990 Bay St • Map K1 • 416 921 9990 • $$$$*

10 La Palette
This bohemian space tempts with good-value French food, and takes its pedigree to heart, offering horse tenderloin to adventurous diners. About 75 types of beers. 🌐 *256 Augusta Ave • Map H2 • 416 929 4900 • $$$*

➡️ ***Note:*** *All restaurants accept credit cards and serve vegetarian meals unless otherwise stated*

Around Town – Downtown

Left **Bedford Academy** Right **This is London**

TOP 10 Bars & Clubs

1 C-Lounge
The spa-inspired C-Lounge's chic patio attracts a hip crowd who come to sip cocktails and lounge in the intimate cabanas around the pool. ⊗ *456 Wellington St W • Map H4 • 416 260 9393*

2 This is London
An upmarket club operating a no-jeans policy and catering to young professionals. There is a full-time make-up artist based in the ladies room. ⊗ *364 Richmond St W • Map J4 • 416 351 1100*

3 Avenue
Unwind at the end of a day's shopping or wheeling-and-dealing as you linger over a cocktail or glass of crisp chardonnay in this chic bar. High people-watching factor *(see p56)*. ⊗ *21 Avenue Rd • Map C2 • 416 964 0411*

4 The Roof Lounge
Snag a seat on the 18th-floor terrace for the view, or savor the warm atmosphere inside while watching a master bartender at work *(see p56)*. ⊗ *4 Avenue Rd • Map C2 • 416 324 1568*

5 Lula Lounge
Sexy salsa gets your hips swaying as rum cocktails loosen you up *(see p57)*. ⊗ *1585 Dundas St W • Map A4 • 416 588 0307 • Adm*

6 Cameron House
Hang out with the locals and catch great music in this ornate yet very casual bar. Celebrities, including Prince, sometimes drop by *(see p56)*. ⊗ *408 Queen St W • Map H3 • 416 703 0811 • Adm to backroom shows*

7 Panorama
Not for acrophobics, this bar's patios, on the 51st floor of the ManuLife Centre, are the city's highest, offering spectacular views. Extensive cocktail list. ⊗ *55 Bloor St W • Map D3 • 416 967 0000 • Adm*

8 Bedford Academy
With 18 beers on tap, reasonably priced cocktails, TVs to catch the sports game, and a lovely patio in summer, it's no wonder this place is popular with students from nearby University of Toronto *(see p76)*. ⊗ *36 Prince Arthur St • Map C3 • 416 921 4600*

9 Souz Dal
A hip crowd sips all manner of martinis to funk beats in this small candlelit room. Wall hangings and a domed ceiling lend a Middle Eastern flair. An enclosed "patio" at back adds a few more seats to this tiny spot. ⊗ *636 College St • Map B3 • 416 537 1883*

10 The Drake Lounge
Recline on a comfy sofa beside the fireplace while taking in the scene, including the Raw Bar peddling its oysters. Then check out the live music or art happening downstairs in the Underground. ⊗ *1150 Queen St W • Map A4 • 416 531 5042*

Around Town – Downtown

Price Categories

Price categories include a three-course meal for one, half a bottle of wine, and all unavoidable extra charges including tax.	**$** under $30
	$$ $30–$50
	$$$ $50–$80
	$$$$ $80–$110
	$$$$$ over $110

Above *Sashimi* and *maki*, Sushi Island

Ethnic Eats

Indian Rice Factory
North Indian cuisine whets the appetite with chickpea and potato *pakoras*, then heats things up with spicy vindaloos and other delectable curries. ✆ *414 Dupont St • Map C2 • 416 961 3472 • $$$*

93 Harbord
Meze are updated in this Middle Eastern standout, with addictive *hummus* and *musakhan* – a mix of chicken, onions, and pine nuts, and mains that include lamb tagine in a fig and shiraz sauce: divine! ✆ *93 Harbord St • Map B3 • 416 922 5914 • $$*

Boulevard Café
The city's oldest Peruvian restaurant offers grilled meats and excellent seafood specialties. *Tapas* and drinks served in the upstairs lounge; in summer, cool off with a sangria on the large, lovely patio. ✆ *161 Harbord St • Map C4 • 416 961 7676 • $$$*

Lee Garden
This Cantonese restaurant is the place to go for tasty chow mein, barbecued pork, and fresh seafood and vegetable dishes. ✆ *331 Spadina Ave • Map H2 • 416 593 9524 • $$*

Banjara
Its unfussy, diner-like interior belies the fine Indian cooking that Banjara has become famous for. Flavors include hints of tart lemon and freshly roasted cumin. ✆ *796 Bloor St W • Map B3 • 416 963 9360 • $*

Korea House
In the heart of Toronto's Koreatown, this family-run restaurant cooks up traditional Korean fare, with starters such as *kimchee* (hot, pickled cabbage) and fish and meat mains. Try the unusual Korean rice wines or *soju*, strong distilled liquors flavored with fruit or flowers. ✆ *666 Bloor St W • Map B3 • 416 536 8666 • $$*

John's Italian Café
Cozy and inviting, with a terrific patio, this café serves Italian classics such as pizza, gnocchi, and simple pastas. ✆ *27 Baldwin St • Map J2 • 416 596 8848 • $*

Sushi Island
This lovely Japanese restaurant draws sushi-lovers from all over the city with perhaps the freshest *sashimi* in town. Noodles, *tempura*, and hot pots are also favorites. ✆ *571 College St • Map B3 • 416 535 1515 • $*

Café Diplomatico
The patio is the place to be at this Little Italy institution *(see p39)*. Panzerotti, pizza, and pasta are on the menu, but it's the people-watching opportunities that draw the crowds. ✆ *594 College St • Map B3 • 416 534 4637 • $*

Spring Rolls
South Asian delights for those on a budget: the Vietnamese *pho* (noodle soup), Thai curries, and stir-fries are excellent value. ✆ *693 Yonge St • Map D3 • 416 972 7655 • $*

Note: *All restaurants accept credit cards and serve vegetarian meals unless otherwise stated*

Left **Vegetables at St. Lawrence Market** Right **Sidewalk café, The Danforth**

East

THE EASTERN PART OF TORONTO *is a region of contrasts. Some of the city's grandest old mansions remain along the stately streets of Jarvis and Sherbourne, though many of these homes were abandoned for years and have only in the past few decades undergone renovation and gentrification.*

The same is true of Cabbagetown, originally a working-class Irish immigrant neighborhood, where Victorian rowhouses and cottages have been transformed into an upscale neighborhood of urban professionals. There are many historic sights in the area and a vibrant streetlife throughout Toronto's east side, thanks to the lively gay village along Church Street, the Greek and Macedonian enclave of The Danforth, and the fresh-food destination of St. Lawrence Market. To the south, a complex of Victorian buildings has been converted into the Distillery Historic District, one of the city's newest shopping and entertainment destinations.

Glass artwork, Ainsley Gallery

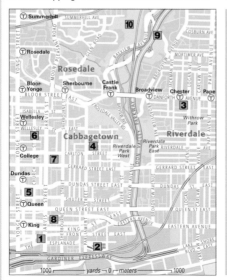

Sights

1. St. Lawrence Market
2. Distillery Historic District
3. The Danforth
4. Cabbagetown
5. Mackenzie House
6. Church Street
7. Allan Gardens
8. Toronto's First Post Office
9. Todmorden Mills Heritage Museum & Art Centre
10. Don Valley Brickworks

Cabbagetown cottage

St. Lawrence Market
Farmers sell fresh produce and baked goods from seasonal stalls in the north market on Saturdays, with many specializing in organic food. In the vibrant south market, open Tuesday to Saturday, permanent vendors sell everything from fresh bread and produce to seafood, meats, and cheeses. The south building served as City Hall in the mid- to late 1800s *(see p86)*. ✎ *Map M4*

Distillery Historic District
This Victorian industrial district is now one of the city's most interesting and picturesque. Pedestrian-only cobblestone streets lead past old warehouses and historic factories stunningly preserved and renovated to house galleries, restaurants, performance venues, and specialty shops *(see pp20–21)*.

The Danforth
Linked to downtown by the 1918 Prince Edward Viaduct, which spans the Don River Valley, The Danforth has been called home by the city's thriving Greek and Macedonian communities since the 1950s. In early August, the weeklong Taste of The Danforth street festival is a smorgasbord of tasty treats and live entertainment *(see p39)*. ✎ *Map F3*

Cabbagetown
One of Toronto's earliest subdivisions, dating to the 1840s, this district remained a working-class community well into the 1970s. Many of the cottages and Victorian homes have since been renovated, and it is now an upscale residential enclave that makes for a pleasant stroll. On the east side is Riverdale Park and its delightful Riverdale Farm *(see p48)*. Across the street, on the grounds of the Necropolis Cemetery, is a chapel built in 1872, a Gothic Revival treasure. At the north end of Cabbagetown, St. James Cemetery, Toronto's oldest, has many beautiful crypts *(see p38)*. ✎ *Map E3–E4*

Mackenzie House
This Greek Revival rowhouse, built in 1858, was the home of Toronto's first mayor, William Lyon Mackenzie, who returned here after being granted amnesty for his leading role in the failed Upper Canada Rebellion in 1837. Now a period museum, it features a recreated printshop and a gallery with changing exhibitions. It is rumored to be haunted. ✎ *82 Bond St • Map L3 • open Jan–Apr: noon–5pm Sat–Sun; May–Sep: noon–5pm Tue–Sun; Sep–Dec: noon–4pm Tue–Fri, noon–5pm Sat–Sun • Adm*

Mackenzie House

*The construction of the Prince Edward Viaduct is featured in Michael Ondaatje's 1987 bestselling novel **In the Skin of a Lion***

6 Church Street

The hub of Toronto's Gay and Lesbian Village, Church Street from Carleton Street to north of Wellesley Street, is vibrant day and night. Bars and restaurants cater to an out crowd, and specialty shops, such as those selling body wear, abound. The general vibe is pink and proud and it's no wonder that the popular TV show *Queer as Folk*, made in Toronto, is often filmed on location at Church Street. Pick up a copy of the free bi-weekly newspaper *Xtra!*, available at most shops on the street, for listings of everything the village has to offer. ◈ *Map L1–L2*

Conservatory, Allan Gardens

Don River

Named by the lieutenant-governor of Upper Canada, John Graves Simcoe, after a stream in Yorkshire, England, the Don River is one of the city's defining natural features. Flowing just east of downtown into Lake Ontario, the river and its steep valley cut a swath through the city. While industrial use of the river, particularly at its southern end – where its meandering course is channeled into an abrupt right turn – have degraded the water, recent naturalization projects have started the long process of restoring the Don Valley to ecological health. The ribbon of connected greenspaces following the Don's course means that you can hike and cycle along bike paths for hours right in the center of the city and encounter few signs of civilization.

7 Allan Gardens

This large park embodies the contradictions of the downtown-eastside: It is both grand and gritty. Best explored during the day, the gardens, which first opened in 1860, contain a delightful glass-and-metal conservatory complex consisting of six greenhouses, each with a different climate zone, built in 1910. Inside, the exuberant displays of seasonal and permanent greenery and flowers delight the senses. ◈ *Map M2*

8 Toronto's First Post Office

This working post office and museum opened in 1833 and is the only surviving example of a British-era post office in Canada. Here, you can write a letter with a quill pen and have it stamped with a distinctive cancellation mark: "York-Toronto 1833." There is also a topographic model of 1830s Toronto, period furniture, and 19th-century reproduction ink wells and sealing wax. The library, housing an extensive archival collection of postal-related materials, is open by appointment only, but admission to the museum is free for self-guided tours. ◈ *260 Adelaide St E • Map M4 • Open 9am–4pm Mon–Fri, 10am–4pm Sat–Sun*

Toronto's First Post Office

Todmorden Mills

9 Todmorden Mills Heritage Museum & Art Centre

The collection of late 18th-century buildings that makes up this museum complex impart the feel of a historic village. Fine examples of the original industrial architecture, such as a paper mill, are peppered throughout the site. Two houses – the 1797 Terry Cottage and 1800s Helliwell House – have been restored with period furnishings. The 1881 Don Train Station will delight rail buffs. The Brewery Gallery exhibits pieces related to the site. A wildflower preserve bursts with trilliums in spring, and trails offer nature lovers lots of wildlife spotting opportunities, but be prepared for deep snow in winter. ◈ 67 Pottery Rd • Map F2 • Museum complex open May–Sep: 11am–4:30pm Tue–Fri, noon–5pm Sat–Sun • Adm • Grounds open year-round

10 Don Valley Brickworks

The smokestack is just one of the historic features that remain at this once-thriving industrial complex, which opened in 1889 to manufacture bricks for local buildings using clay found on site. Some 100 years later, the quarry has been returned to nature as a park with ponds and meadows (see p40). ◈ 550 Bayview Ave • Map E2

A Cabbagetown Stroll

Morning

Begin your day with an espresso at **Jet Fuel**, 519 Parliament St. After your caffeine jolt, turn right and walk north to **Wellesley St**, then turn right again and walking east to take in the charming Victorian architecture. Note the strange animal and face carvings on **No. 314**. Explore the lanes running northward, including **Wellesley Cottages**, a courtyard tucked behind the street with seven gabled cottages. As you come to the end of Wellesley St, spend a few moments wandering through **Wellesley Park**, enjoying the view across the Don Valley.

Backtrack to Wellesley St and turn left onto **Sumach St**, its charming houses classic Cabbagetown. Note Second Empire-style **No. 420–422**, built in 1886, and the English cottage style of **Nos. 404–408**. Turn left at Winchester St; **Necropolis Cemetery**, Toronto's oldest non-denominational graveyard, will be on the left. Peek into the **chapel** to admire the stained-glass windows.

Afternoon

For lunch, head back along Winchester St to Parliament St, turning left to Carlton St, where you'll find the **Town Grill** at No. 243.

After lunch, continue to meander the area's compact streets – Metcalfe, Salisbury, and Sackville – before walking east to **Riverdale Park** and its **Riverdale Farm** (see p48). Across the street from the park's northwest corner is cute **Winchester Café**, dispensing refreshments through a side window.

Left **South Market** Right **Outdoor vendors, North Market**

St. Lawrence Market

South Market
Opened in 1844 as Toronto's second City Hall, this building had a police station on the first floor and a jail in the basement. Today it houses a thriving public market – and some of the tastiest, freshest meats, cheese, produce, and breads around.
◈ 91 Front St E • Open 8am–6pm Tue–Thu, 8am–7pm Fri, 5am–5pm Sat

North Market
Buy fruits, vegetables, and herbs directly from those who grow them. Organic items and home-baked treats, too. ◈ 92 Front St E • Open 5am–early afternoon Sat

Outdoor Stands
Sprawling on the sidewalks outside the North Market, these produce and flower stalls only add to the boisterous atmosphere of market Saturdays. For the best selection, arrive early in the morning.

Toronto Dollars
Trade Canadian money at the South Market booth for Toronto Dollars, an alternative currency accepted by many market merchants. Ten percent of each dollar used is donated to local projects.

Montreal Bagels
Locals love St. Urbain Bakery's dense, chewy buns, in the South Market. The bagel-cooking method – boil then bake in a wood-fired oven – hails from French-Canadian city Montreal.

Alex Farms
A cheese lover's paradise, in South Market, selling every kind of cheese imaginable, from French cantal to the most pungent of blues. Good raw-milk cheese selection.

Buskers and Craft-Sellers
Lively street action is part of the charm of market Saturdays, as buskers entertain and craftspeople ply their wares outside both the north and south buildings.

Peameal Bacon Sandwiches
Quintessentially Canadian, and perfect to fuel up for the day, the kaiser buns at South Market's Carousel Bakery are stuffed with salty, peameal-encrusted pork.

Market Gallery
Artifacts and photographs of Toronto's history are exhibited in free, themed shows, in the old council chamber tucked on the second floor of the South Market. See the market from a different perspective, through the large window looking out onto the floor. ◈ Open 10am–4pm Wed–Fri, 9am–4pm Sat, noon–4pm Sun

St. Lawrence Hall
Just north of the market, at Jarvis and King streets, is this magnificent Victorian building, a carved stone and cast-iron gem. Built in 1850 for grand public gatherings, it is now used for private functions.

Several pay-parking lots are near the market; the two closest are on Jarvis St south of Front, and on Market St south of the Esplanade

Left **Lileo** Right **Ethel**

🔟 Shopping East

Sophie's Lingerie
Lingerie, especially for fuller figures – from top designers such as Lejaby and La Perla, in a wide range of colors and sexy designs. Expert fitting. 🔌 *527 Danforth Ave • Map F3 • 416 461 6113*

The Cook's Place
Copper pots, trendy gadgets, silicon baking forms, Japanese knives – this store has everything the gourmet cook needs or desires. 🔌 *488 Danforth Ave • Map F3 • 416 461 5211*

Carrot Common
Lovers of organic foods and natural body care shop happily here at this 17-store complex dedicated to eco-friendly products. Recharge with a sampling of the delicious prepared foods on offer here. 🔌 *320 & 348 Danforth Ave • Map F3 • 416 466 2129*

Soma Chocolate
A store for the chocolate cognoscenti. Sample the divine confections or try a cup of steaming Mayan hot chocolate, redolent with spices. 🔌 *55 Mill St, Bldg 48 • Map E5 • 416 815 7662*

Lileo
A fashion, wellness, and self-discovery store. Yoga togs, Ayurvedic body lotions, handbags, books, CDs, and limited-edition running shoes. A juice bar with a raw-food menu helps keep shoppers' appetites at bay. 🔌 *55 Mill St, Bldg 35 • Map E5 • 416 413 1410*

Applause
Audiophiles lust after the high-end components sold here. Owner and sound-guru Rob will also give you a square deal on the used equipment. 🔌 *758 Queen St E • Map F4 • 416 465 7649*

Ethel
Elegant teak buffets and dining tables, glass and acrylic coffee tables, and other nifty pieces from the 1960s and 1970s, at reasonable prices. 🔌 *1091 Queen St E • Map F4 • 416 778 6608*

Festoon
The husband and wife team behind this quirky home decor and gift shop are well travelled, and it shows. Find unique and playful treasures from around the world. 🔌 *1101 Queen St E • Map F4 • 416 461 4495*

Kristapsons
Pacific salmon, cold-smoked on the premises using a secret recipe, is all you'll find in this store – but what a find. Those in the know claim it ranks among the world's best. 🔌 *1095 Queen St E • Map F4 • 416 466 5152*

Henry's
Everything a photographer needs, from the latest digital cameras to vintage Leica lenses, and necessities such as film, batteries, photo paper, and a quality developing service. Knowledgeable, helpful staff. 🔌 *119 Church St • Map L4 • 416 868 0872*

Left **Dora Keogh** Right **Jamie Kennedy Wine Bar**

Bars & Pubs

1 Consort Bar
Relish the great whiskeys and masterfully mixed cocktails in this dignified bar in the Royal Meridien Hotel. ◈ 37 King St E • Map L4 • 416 863 3131

2 Betty's
This friendly pub, popular with locals, offers beers on tap, tasty food such as burgers and Montreal smoked meat on a bun, billiard tables, and a great patio. ◈ 240 King St E • Map M4 • 416 368 1300

3 Barrio
Candlelight and soft music combine with a good drinks list and inspired food served in small portions, tapas style. ◈ 896 Queen St E • Map F4 • 416 572 0600

4 C'est What?
A casual spot with 45 microbrews on tap, some, such as the hemp, rye, and coffee brews, produced exclusively for the pub. Ethnic dishes. ◈ 67 Front St E • Map L5 • 416 867 9499

5 Irish Embassy Pub and Grill
Savor a drink at the bar or delicious pub food featuring Irish specialities while sitting on a comfy banquette. The high ceilings and big windows keep it airy. ◈ 49 Yonge St • Map L5 • 416 866 8282

6 Dora Keogh
A reconstructed 1890s Irish pub, with a fireplace, and cozy nooks and crannies. Good selection of beers and, of course,

whiskeys. Live Irish music is presented occasionally. ◈ 141 Danforth Ave • Map F3 • 416 778 1804

7 Allen's
An endless selection of global beers and distillations, plus top Celtic music acts and a friendly vibe. ◈ 143 Danforth Ave • Map F3 • 416 463 3086

8 Imperial Public Library
Regulars, students, and old-timers treasure the circular bar and jukeboxes playing big-band hits in this no-frills place. ◈ 58 Dundas St E • Map L3 • 416 977 4667

9 Myth
A long, stylish bar and unusual decor of myth-inspired objects. Mediterranean food, and, in summer, a great sidewalk patio. ◈ 417 Danforth Ave • Map F3 • 416 461 8383

10 BeerBistro
Beer is taken seriously here with an enormous selection, a beer school, and Wednesday happy-hour tastings. Many menu items incorporate beers too. ◈ 18 King St E • Map L4 • 416 861 9872

Ontario microbreweries include Steam Whistle, Creemore, Brick, Lakeport, Lakes of Muskoka, Neustadt Springs, and Niagara Falls

Above **Rosewater Supper Club**

🔟 Restaurants

1 Café Brussel
Some 30 preparations of mussels (all with excellent *frites*) and other delightful Belgian dishes. 🔊 *124 Danforth Ave • Map F3 • 416 465 7363 • $$$$*

2 Verveine
Contemporary French cuisine and excellent brunches are the draw at this Leslieville favorite *(see p54)*. 🔊 *1097 Queen St E • Map F4 • 416 405 9906 • $$$*

3 Jamie Kennedy Wine Bar
Local organic ingredients are featured at top chef Jamie Kennedy's intimate wine bar. Tapas-sized servings are conducive to sharing. 🔊 *9 Church St • Map L5 • 416 362 5586 • $$$*

4 Perigee
A nightly tasting menu – French, with a Mediterranean twist – delights gourmets in the Distillery Historic District. Chef Pat Riley genially rules the open kitchen. 🔊 *55 Mill St, Bldg 59 • Map E5 • 416 364 1397 • $$$$$*

5 Starfish
Seafood is given graceful, luscious treatment here. Outstanding oysters. 🔊 *100 Adelaide St E • Map M4 • 416 366 7827 • $$$*

6 Biff's
The elegant atmosphere – zinc bar, banquettes, large mirrors – matches the classic French bistro fare. 🔊 *4 Front St E • Map L5 • 416 860 0086 • $$$$*

7 Pappas Grill
This boisterous Greek taverna pleases with excellent starter dips and filling mains such as roast lamb and souvlaki. 🔊 *440 Danforth Ave • Map F3 • 416 469 9595 • $*

8 Rosewater Supper Club
Inventive French-style cuisine, in a beautifully restored Victorian building. Along with the dining room and lower-level supper club are three intimate bars, including a cigar lounge. 🔊 *19 Toronto St • Map L4 • 416 214 5888 • $$$$*

9 Hiro Sushi
Diners feast on grilled tuna, *sashimi*, *wasabi*-spiked fish, and other Japanese delights, accompanied by fine sakes. 🔊 *171 King St E • Map M4 • 416 304 0550 • $$$*

10 Gio Rana's Really, Really Nice Restaurant
This unconventionally named and decorated restaurant (a huge plaster nose hangs outside the former bank) specializes in great-value southern Italian fare. Open kitchen. 🔊 *1220 Queen St E • Map B2 • 416 469 5225 • $$*

Note: *All restaurants accept credit cards and serve vegetarian meals unless otherwise stated*

Left **Ashbridges Bay Park, The Beach** Right **Canada's Wonderland**

Greater Toronto

THE AREA SURROUNDING THE CITY PROPER *has expanded rapidly in the last few decades, with suburban bedroom communities popping up around the urban fringe, engulfing fertile farmland. While highway development ensures convenient access to the many sites outside the city, roads can be extremely crowded at rush hour, and it is a good idea to plan excursions for off-peak times. Many delightful parks and natural areas lie just outside the city, along with spacious beaches. Toronto Zoo, set in the huge wilderness area of Rouge Park (see p41) on the eastern edge of the city, is a delightful place to spend a day, as is, for family thrills, Canada's Wonderland. Several historic attractions, such as Black Creek Pioneer Village, where costumed guides demonstrate pioneer life, or Bradley Museum, a restored farmhouse, provide a glimpse into mid-19th-century country life. Art lovers are drawn due north to the renowned McMichael Canadian Art Collection in the charming village of Kleinburg.*

Polar bear, Toronto Zoo

🔟 Sights

1. McMichael Canadian Art Collection
2. Toronto Zoo
3. The Beach
4. Canada's Wonderland
5. Ontario Science Centre
6. Black Creek Pioneer Village
7. Gibson House Museum
8. Colborne Lodge
9. Bradley Museum
10. Toronto Aerospace Museum

Sign up for DK's email newsletter on traveldk.com

White Pine, McMichael Collection

1 McMichael Canadian Art Collection

Located in Kleinburg, 18 miles (30 km) from downtown Toronto, this outstanding gallery features a stellar display of works by the seminal Group of Seven painters, their contemporaries such as Tom Thomson and Emily Carr, and the artists they inspired. The gallery also exhibits an impressive collection of First Nations and Inuit artists. ◈ *10365 Islington Ave, Kleinburg • Map A1 • 905 893 1121 • Open May–Oct: 10am–5pm daily; Nov–Apr: 10am–4pm • Adm*

2 Toronto Zoo

You will want a full day to explore this 710-acre (287-ha) zoo and its some 5,000 animals representing about 450 species. Roaming freely within outdoor enclosures, large creatures such as African elephants can be seen along 6 miles (10 km) of trails. Also along the trails are four tropical pavilions, each representing a distinct geographic habitat. ◈ *361A Old Finch Ave • Map B1 • 416 392 5929 • Open Mar–Apr & Sep–Oct: 9am–6pm daily; May–Aug: 9am–7:30pm daily; Oct–Mar: 9:30am–4:30pm daily • Adm*

3 The Beach

This is one area of the city that takes full advantage of its lakeside setting, with an atmosphere that feels more like a small resort town. In summer especially, crowds throng to the white sand beaches, stroll the 2.5-mile (4-km) boardwalk, picnic in Kew Gardens, a turn-of-the-19-century park, and shop along Queen Street *(see p93)*. The area is at its busiest best in late July, during the Beaches international jazz festival *(see p47)*.◈ *Map B2*

4 Canada's Wonderland

This theme park north of Toronto draws crowds with its more than 50 rides, huge water park, and live entertainment. Thrills abound, the biggest pleasers being the roller coasters. ◈ *9580 Jane St, Vaughan • Map A1 • 905 832 8131 • Open May 1–Victoria Day: 10am–8pm Sat–Sun; Victoria Day–Labour Day: 10am–10pm daily; Labour Day–Thanksgiving: 10am–8pm Sat–Sun • Adm*

5 Ontario Science Centre

Exhibits in this museum are interactive and geared toward youngsters, all in the name of making science education fun. Eleven themed areas cover a diverse range of topics, including Earth's ecosystems, space, sport, communication, energy, and the human body.◈ *770 Don Mills Rd • Map B1 • 416 696 1000 • Open 10am–5pm daily • Adm*

Ontario Science Centre

6 Black Creek Pioneer Village

For an authentic taste of early settler life, visit this re-creation of a 19th-century rural Ontario community. Among the dozens of buildings – a handful original to the site, the rest moved here and restored – are a school, a church, village shops, houses, and barns. The grounds include an orchard, millpond, restored gardens, and grazing livestock. Costumed staff demonstrate pioneer crafts and carry out tasks such as tinsmithing and milling flour (the flour is available for sale). Free wagon rides are popular with the kids. ◎ 1000 Murray Ross Pkwy, Downsview • Map A1 • 416 736 1733 • Open May–Jun: 9:30am–4:30pm Mon–Fri, 11am–5pm Sat–Sun; Jul–Labour Day: 10am–5pm Mon–Fri, 11am–5pm Sat–Sun; Labour Day–Dec 31: 9:30am–4pm Mon–Fri, 11am–4:30pm Sat–Sun • Adm

7 Gibson House Museum

While North York is a relentlessly modern part of the city, it is also home to this historic gem – an elegant Georgian farmhouse built in 1851. The original owner, land surveyor and mapper David

Black Creek Pioneer Village

Gibson, was a leader of the Upper Canada Rebellion in 1837 who was forced to flee to the US when the uprising failed. Following his pardon, Gibson returned and built this home for his wife and seven children. The museum hosts guided tours and also holds classes in such forgotten arts as hearth-cooking. ◎ 5172 Yonge St • Map A1 • 416 395 7432 • Open Oct–Aug: noon–5pm Tue–Sun • Adm

8 Colborne Lodge

This 1837 house was the residence of land surveyor John Howard and his wife, Jemima. Howard deeded the estate to the city, thereby forming the basis for High Park (see p40). Located at the south end of the park, the Regency-style house, with its gorgeous circular verandah, has been fully restored and includes many of the Howards' original belongings, including John Howard's original watercolors of early Toronto scenes. Costumed guides lead tours. Don't miss the garden, planted with kitchen herbs and flowers. Seasonal celebrations, such as the Harvest Festival and the lamplit processions at Christmastime, are particularly popular. ◎ Colborne Lodge Dr • Map A2 • 416 392 6916 • Open Jan–Apr: noon–4pm Sat–Sun; May–Sep: noon–5pm Tue–Sun; Oct–Dec: noon–4pm Tue–Sun • Adm

R. C. Harris Filtration Plant

Built in the late 1930s, in an era when public works buildings were grand statements – expressions of engineering mastery – this filtration plant has been dubbed the "palace of purification." Monumentally perched atop a gentle hill, this Art Deco structure holds the machines that treat the city's drinking water, which is pumped into the facility from a pipe that begins 1.5 miles (3 km) offshore, in Lake Ontario. Close to 200 million gallons (757 million litres) of water are processed daily, supplying about half of Toronto's needs.

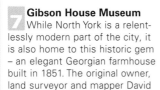

Bradley Museum

This collection of early-19th-century buildings offers a window on the past. The 1830 farmhouse was built by Lewis and Elizabeth Bradley, United Empire Loyalists who left the US and settled in Ontario, raising seven children. The restored house features period artifacts. The Anchorage, also on the grounds, is a Regency-style cottage originally home to Royal Navy officer John Skynner. It offers rotating exhibitions and, the last Sunday of the month, afternoon tea. *1620 Orr Rd, Mississauga • Map A2 • 905 615 4860 • Open 1–5pm Sun; Jul–Aug: 1–5pm Wed–Sun • Adm • Bradley House not wheelchair accessible*

Toronto Aerospace Museum

Housed in the 1929 de Havilland Aircraft of Canada building on the grounds of the former Downsview Airport – an air-force base now being converted to a public park – this museum celebrates Canada's aviation history. Along with archival photos, it exhibits artifacts and full-sized aircraft, such as the 1950s jet trainer and an anti-submarine aircraft built for the Royal Canadian Navy. Particularly unusual are the exhibits of flight-training simulators used for pilot instruction in the 1940s and 1950s. *65 Carl Hall Rd • Map A1 • 416 638 6078 • Open 10am–4pm Thu–Sat, noon–4pm Sun • Adm*

Toronto Aerospace Museum

A Day at the Beach

Morning

Begin at **Sunset Grill**, 2006 Queen St E, for breakfast. (The waffles are a local favorite.) Fortified, cross the street and meander toward the lake through **Kew Gardens**, noting the unusual circular path and rounded windows of **Kew Williams Cottage**, built in 1902, at the park's south end. If you prefer cycling to walking, first check out **Beach Cycles** (1882 Queen St E) for equipment rental.

Reaching the **boardwalk**, turn right and follow it to the end, a 15 minute stroll. Look out for the paved path on the right; take it into **Ashbridges Bay Park**, where you can stroll along the waterfront, watching sailboats moor. The city view from the west side of the park is excellent.

For lunch, retrace your steps to Kew Gardens, then up to Queen St, for a famously good burger at **Lick's** (No. 1960).

Afternoon

Spend the afternoon browsing the shops on Queen St, picking up at treat at **The Nutty Chocolatier**, No. 2179, to enjoy while taking a break at the serene sunken rock garden – **Ivan Forest Gardens** – at Queen St E and Glen Manor Dr.

Shopped out, snag a seat on **Quigley's** patio (No. 2232) and relax with a refreshment. If you're up for more walking, continue another 10 minutes east to the **R. C. Harris Filtration Plant** *(see p92)* to stroll the grounds of this Art Deco gem and admire the view of the Scarborough Bluffs *(see p94)* and Lake Ontario.

Left **Bluffer's Park** Right **Humber Arboretum**

🔟 Greenspaces

1 Rouge Park
North America's largest urban park, home to the wildest natural area in the city, follows the course of the Rouge River. Many hiking trails. ◈ *Map B1 • 905 713 6038*

2 Kortright Center
This premier conservation area hosts hands-on activities and guided nature walks for all ages – the nighttime "owl prowls" are very popular. Some 11 miles (18 km) of trails lead through forests, meadows, and Humber River valleylands. ◈ *9550 Pine Valley Dr, Woodbridge • Map A1 • 905 832 2289 • Adm*

3 Toronto Botanical Garden
Magnificent floral displays are to be found in this large park by the Wilket Creek ravine. Kids' activities at the superb teaching garden. ◈ *777 Lawrence Ave E • Map B1 • 416 397 1340*

4 High Park
Toronto's largest downtown park has extensive trails through woodlands and oak savanna, along with playgrounds, tennis courts, a small zoo, historic Colborne Lodge *(see p92)*, and a snack bar and restaurant. ◈ *1873 Bloor St W • Map A2*

5 Bluffer's Park
Dramatic sandstone cliffs rise 350 ft (110 m) above Lake Ontario, providing a spectacular backdrop to this east-end park. Marina and seasonal snack bar. ◈ *Brimley Rd, south end • Map B2*

6 Guildwood Park
Enjoy gardens and naturalized areas full of woodland wildflowers at this Scarborough Bluff park. Intriguing architectural artifacts saved from demolished buildings dot the grounds. ◈ *201 Guildwood Pkwy • Map B1 • 416 392 1111*

7 Humber Bay Butterfly Habitat
Native flowers and shrubs attract butterflies at this lakeshore park with a great view of the city's skyline. A demonstration garden highlights butterfly-attracting flowers for home gardens. ◈ *Humber Bay Park Rd E • Map A2 • 416 392 1339*

8 Sunnybrook Park
Encompassing shady Burke Ravine and two forests, this park provides respite from summer heat. Interpretive nature trails; riding stables; several sports fields; picnic tables and restaurant. ◈ *Enter west of Leslie St via Wilket Creek Park • Map B1*

9 Martin Goodman Trail
Hugging Lake Ontario, the 12-mile (22 km) trail connects the waterfront parks and is popular with joggers, cyclists, and in-line skaters. ◈ *Map A2–B2*

10 Humber Arboretum
Set near the West Humber River, this nature center has self-guided trails through woodlands and meadows, and fine exhibits on plants and wildlife. ◈ *205 Humber College Blvd • Map A2*

Some parks close at dusk; call ahead to confirm hours. For more information on Toronto's parks, visit the website www.trca.on.ca

Price Categories

Price categories include a three-course meal for one, half a bottle of wine, and all unavoidable extra charges including tax.

$	under $30
$$	$30–$50
$$$	$50–$80
$$$$	$80–$110
$$$$$	over $110

Above **Auberge du Pommier**

Restaurants

Amaya
Fresh textures and subtle spicing define the nouveau Indian cuisine at Amaya. Start off with the signature curry martini. *1701 Bayview Ave • Map B2 • 416 322 3270 • $$*

Scaramouche
The Pasta Bar is a Toronto institution – and less pricey than the elegant main dining room, which has been serving up inventive, consistently excellent cuisine for decades. Fabulous view of the city. *1 Benvenuto Pl • Map C2 • 416 961 8011• $$$$ main room; $$$ Pasta Bar*

Grano
A cheerful, boisterous place with excellent, satisfying, Italian fare and a family atmosphere. There are lots of vegetarian options on the menu. *2035 Yonge St • Map B2 • 416 440 1986 • $$$*

North 44°
Chef Mark McEwan dishes up modern international cooking – French classics with sophisticated twists. An impressive drinks and wine list. *2537 Yonge St • Map B1 • 416 487 4897 • $$$$$*

Via Allegro
Authentic Italian food – pasta, seafood, and wood-fired oven pizzas – and an award-winning wine cellar which, with over 3,000 selections, is an oenophile magnet. *1750 The Queensway • Map A2 • 416 622 6677 • $$$$*

Sushi Kaji
Set menu options – including the deluxe, chef's choice *omakase* menu – present course after course of wonderful, complex Japanese creations balanced with simple, incredibly fresh, *sashimi* and sushi. *860 The Queensway • Map A2 • 416 252 2166 • $$$$*

Auberge du Pommier
Classic French cooking with a contemporary twist. Two intimate rooms, a bar, and a small patio. In winter, ask for a table by the fireplace. *4150 Yonge St • Map B1 • 416 222 2220 • $$$$*

Dragon Dynasty
Classic Chinese dishes more than make up for the unpromising surroundings of this restaurant, located in a mall. *2301 Brimley Rd • Map B1 • 416 321 9000 • $$$*

Katsura
Japanese specialties such as sushi, *sashimi, tempura*, and grilled fish. Diners can sit at the sushi bar, around *teppan* tables in the dining room, or in private *tatami* rooms. *900 York Mills Rd • Map B1 • 416 444 2511 • $$$$*

Pomegranate
Reservations are essential at this popular Persian gem, where elaborate rice dishes are topped with rich sauces and aromatic flatbreads. A good wine list, traditional Persian furnishing, and music are other features. *420 College St • Map B3 • 416 921 7557 • $$*

Note: *All restaurants accept credit cards and serve vegetarian meals unless otherwise stated*

Left **Horseshoe Falls, Niagara Falls** Right **Windmill in Goderich**

Beyond Toronto

WITHIN EASY DRIVING DISTANCE OF TORONTO *are many delightful communities worthy of a daytrip or a more extended visit. North of the city, Honey Harbour and Gravenhurst are the gateways to cottage country, with beautiful lakes and forests, while Collingwood offers excellent skiing in winter and summer fun on Georgian Bay. To the west of Toronto are many charming small towns, such as Stratford, with its world-renowned Shakespearean theater festival, and the Mennonite community of St. Jacobs. Further west, along the shores of Lake Huron, wide sandy beaches stretching north and south of the lovely town of Goderich beckon. The Niagara Peninsula, south and east, can easily fill a weekend, with attractions such as Niagara Falls and Ontario's best wine country, charming inns, and award-winning restaurants.*

Mennonite horse and buggy, St. Jacobs

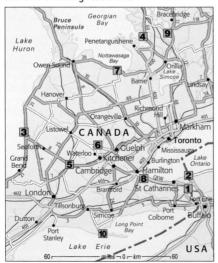

Sights

1. Niagara Falls
2. Niagara-on-the-Lake
3. Goderich
4. Georgian Bay Islands National Park
5. Stratford
6. St. Jacobs and Elora
7. Collingwood
8. Royal Botanical Gardens
9. Gravenhurst
10. Long Point Provincial Park

Sign up for DK's email newsletter on traveldk.com

Queen Street, Niagara-on-the-Lake

1 Niagara Falls
While the town itself sends kitsch to new heights, the falls are spectacular – truly a natural wonder and well worth the trip *(see pp28–31)*.

2 Niagara-on-the-Lake
This charming historic town looks much as it did when built in the early to mid-1800s. Beautiful Georgian and Neo-Classical homes and quaint shops reward leisurely exploration. History buffs won't want to miss the Niagara Historical Museum, with exhibits on the region's fascinating past. The town is a good base for excursions along the scenic Niagara Parkway and to excellent wineries *(see p100)*. In summer, it is home to the Shaw Festival. ◈ *Map Q3 • Niagara Historical Museum: 43 Castlereagh St • 905 468 3912 • Open May–Oct: 10am–5:30pm daily; Nov–Apr: 1–5:30pm daily • Adm*

3 Goderich
Founded in 1827, this town on the shores of Lake Huron has a rich marine history and fine Victorian architecture. Its downtown streets radiate from an unusual octagonal "square," at the center of which is the town hall (1890). The Huron County Museum has a superb collection of old farm equipment and military artifacts. Other stops of interest include the Huron Historic Gaol, a jail built 1839–42; an 1847 lighthouse; and a marine museum in an old lake freighter, open seasonally. ◈ *Map N2 • Huron County Museum: 110 North St, Open 10am–4:30pm Mon–Sat, 1–4:30pm Sun year-round except Labour Day–Victoria Day: closed Sat • Huron Historic Gaol: 181 Victoria St N, Open Victoria Day–Labour Day: 10am–4:30pm daily, Adm*

4 Georgian Bay Islands National Park
Georgian Bay's rugged landscape is characterized by the windswept rock and pine trees of the Canadian Shield. Thousands of islands – some just mounds of granite – dot the Bay; 59 of them make up the park. Access to the largest island, Beausoleil, with its hiking trails, sandy beaches, forest, and the largest variety of reptiles and amphibians of any national park in Canada, is via a 40-minute water taxi ride from the town of Honey Harbour. ◈ *Map P1 • Georgian Bay Islands National Park: 1 888 773 8888*

Moored boats, Georgian Bay

For information about the Shaw Festival, call 1 800 511 7429, or visit its website at www.shawfest.com

Festival Theatre, Stratford

5 Stratford

Known worldwide for its Shakespeare festival, the city continues the theme of the bard with, among other things, a garden planted with every species named in his plays. Riverside parks are picnic-perfect; shops sell works by local artisans. Check out local history at Stratford-Perth Museum, and a fine example of High Victorian architecture – Perth County Court House (1887). ◈ *Map P2*

6 St. Jacobs and Elora

Arts and crafts, antiques, and gift shops set in 19th-century buildings; bakeries; and cozy restaurants abound in these historic villages. St. Jacobs' two markets have hundreds of flea-market and produce stalls – including those offering the area's specialty, maple syrup, sold by local Mennonites. For more on this sweet treat, visit the Maple Syrup Museum at 1441 King St N, St. Jacobs. A 15-mile (24-km) drive northeast is Elora, on the bank of the Grand River and stunning Elora Gorge. ◈ *Map P2 • Farmers' & Flea Market: Farmers' Market Rd, St. Jacobs • Open year-round 7am–3:30pm Thu & Sat and Jun–Labour Day: 8am–3pm Tue*

7 Collingwood

This city takes full advantage of Niagara Escarpment scenery. Nearby Blue Mountain, a high point of the escarpme nt before it dips to lake level at Collingwood, is Ontario's best ski hill. At Scenic Caves Nature Adventures,

Mennonite Country

St. Jacobs is the heart of Ontario's Old Order Mennonite community. Horse-drawn buggies carrying farmers in dark suits and wide-brimmed black hats, the women in aprons and bonnets, share the road with motor vehicles, and illustrate the way of life of this Anabaptist sect. Shunning modern technology, electricity, and the military, they began settling here in 1799, after immigrating to the US from Europe, where they were persecuted for their beliefs.

walk Ontario's longest suspension footbridge, set high in the treetops, or explore the limestone and ice caves. ◈ *Map P1 • Blue Mountain Ski Resort: 705 445 0231 • Scenic Caves Nature Adventures: 705 446 0256*

8 Royal Botanical Gardens

Four nature sanctuaries are replete with greenhouses, cultivated gardens, and trails. In spring, the world's largest lilac collection bursts into bloom. Centuries-old roses thrive summer to fall. In winter, visitors get their fix at the indoor Mediterranean Garden. Gift shop, café, and teahouses (seasonal). ◈ *Map P3 • 680 Plains Rd W, Burlington • Open 9am–dusk daily*

Maple syrup stand, St. Jacobs Market

Stratford's Shakespeare festival runs April to November; call 1 800 567 1600 for details

9 Gravenhurst

The city of Gravenhurst is a good base from which to explore the Muskoka region. It is also the point of departure for lake cruises aboard an 1887 steamship – the oldest operating steamship in North America. Stretching from Algonquin Park to Georgian Bay, Muskoka has over 1,600 lakes and rivers and is a fantastic summer destination. Hundreds of beaches offer excellent swimming opportunities; boats can be rented at launches throughout the region; outfitters organize canoe trips to secluded areas. ⊗ Map Q1 • Muskoka Fleet lake cruises: 705 687 6667

Bethune House, Gravenhurst

10 Long Point Provincial Park

This world-renowned refuge for migrating birds, especially waterfowl, has been recognized by the United Nations as a biosphere reserve. Formed over thousands of years by sand washed from Lake Erie's shoreline, the 25-mile (40-km) sand spit has white sand beaches; the lake's shallow depth ensures warm water throughout the swimming season. Spring and fall are excellent for bird-watching; miles of trails through dunes, forests, wetlands, and grasslands can be enjoyed year-round. Campsites are equipped with showers, laundry facilities, and electrical hook-up. ⊗ Map P3 • Hwy 59, 6 miles (10 km) south of Port Rowan • 519 586 2133

A Drive in the Country

Morning

Start at **St. Jacobs Farmers' and Flea Markets**, admiring the handicrafts, collectibles, and foodstuffs of over 600 vendors. After stocking up snacks, walk across the parking lot to the **Trolley Shop** for a 75-minute horse-drawn trolley tour through Mennonite farm country (Apr–Oct).

After the tour, drive to the **Visitor Centre** at 1406 King St N; it features a short video on Mennonite history, photo exhibits, and a replica of a Mennonite Meetinghouse. Then, ready for lunch, head to **Stone Crock** (No. 1396), for a country-style buffet.

Afternoon

Drive east on County Road 17; in a few miles you'll come to Road 22. Turn north to Route 86, then east on 86, watching for the sign to **West Montrose**. In this small town, look for the last remaining covered bridge in Ontario – called the kissing bridge by locals. The bridge crosses Grand River, a Heritage Waterway. Take Route 23 (turning into R21) north to charming **Elora**, 10 minutes away.

Once there, browse in the craft and antique shops and admire the old limestone buildings before walking to the **Elora Gorge Conservation Area** to swim, hike, and enjoy your picnic snacks by the water.

Next, it's a short drive on Route 18 to **Fergus**, rich in Scottish history and late 19th-century architecture. Dine at the 1860s **Breadalbane Inn** (487 St Andrew St W).

Left **Peller Estates Winery** Right **Carriage House, Vineland Estates Winery**

🔟 Wineries

Vineland Estates Winery
One of the most attractive wineries in the region, this vineyard has an 1857 stone carriage house; two excellent restaurants, one headed by chef Mark Picone *(see p101)*; and guided tours and tastings. ◈ *3620 Moyer Rd, Vineland • Map Q3 • 1 888 846 3526*

Peller Estates Winery
Three generations of winemakers are behind this vineyard, though the facility itself has been recently built. Tours include a peek at the barrel-aging cellar. There is also a restaurant and shop.
◈ *290 John St E, Niagara-on-the-Lake • Map Q3 • 1 888 673 5537*

Hillebrand Estates Winery
Along with estate tours and tastings, Hillebrand hosts specialty events, such as wine country cycling tours (May to October) and an icewine festival (January).
◈ *1249 Niagara Stone Rd, Niagara-on-the-Lake • Map Q3 • 1 800 582 8412*

Peninsula Ridge Estates Winery
The winemaker from Chablis, France, creates interesting blends; the whites are especially good. The restaurant is set in a lovely Victorian house. ◈ *5600 King St W, Beamsville • Map Q3 • 905 563 0900*

Inniskillin Wines
One of Ontario's oldest quality vineyards, established in 1975 and famous for its icewines, has guided and self-guided tours. The shop and tasting bar are in a 1920s barn. ◈ *Line 3, Service Rd 66, Niagara-on-the-Lake • Map Q3 • 1 888 466 4754*

Jackson-Triggs Vinters
One of the most technologically advanced facilities in the region. Tours and tastings. ◈ *2145 Niagara Stone Rd, Niagara-on-the-Lake • Map Q3 • 905 468 4637*

Thirty Bench Wines
This small winery produces outstanding chardonnays and Rieslings. Tastings held in a rustic building. ◈ *4281 Mountainview Rd, Beamsville • Map Q3 • 905 563 1698*

Malivoire Wine Company
In a region known primarily for its white wines, this organic vineyard produces excellent reds. A tasting room is set amid huge production tanks. ◈ *4260 King St E, Beamsville • Map Q3 • 1 866 644 2244*

Reif Estate Winery
This family winery has 135 acres (55 ha) of scenic vineyards. The boutique is in an 1830s cottage. Daily tours in summer.
◈ *15608 Niagara Pkwy, Niagara-on-the-Lake • Map Q3 • 905 468 7738*

Château des Charmes
This family vineyard boasts over five generations of wine-growing experience, with ancestral roots in Frances's Alsace region. A tasting bar, shop, and splendid rose garden. ◈ *1025 York Rd, Niagara-on-the-Lake • Map Q3 • 905 262 4219*

Many vineyards keep seasonal hours; phone ahead to confirm opening and closing times

Price Categories

Price categories include a three-course meal for one, half a bottle of wine, and all unavoidable extra charges including tax.	$ under $30
	$$ $30–$50
	$$$ $50–$80
	$$$$ $80–$110
	$$$$$ over $110

Above **Rundles**

🔟 Restaurants

Eigensinn Farm
Superstar chef Michael Stadländer creates an unparalleled experience that books up months in advance. Intimately gathered in Stadländer's farmhouse, diners feast on exquisite multiple courses showcasing organic ingredients, many of them raised, grown, or foraged on the farm. ✆ *RR 2, Singhampton • Map P1 • 519 922 3128 • Bring your own wine • $$$$$*

Rundles
Classics such as grilled chicken and poached salmon, as well as a more adventurous three-course gourmet menu please at this Stratford institution. ✆ *9 Cobourg St, Stratford • Map P2 • 519 271 6442 • Open May–Oct • $$$$$*

Bailey's
Casual fine-dining amid small-town charm. The diverse selection of meat, fish, and pasta changes daily. Known for its clam chowder. ✆ *120 The Square, Goderich • Map N2 • 519 524 5166 • $$$*

The Compleat Angler
As the name suggests, seafood is the specialty – though there's steak, too. Try the local Great Lakes catch. ✆ *114 Medora St, Port Carling • Map Q1 • 1 877 483 5050 • Open Easter to Thanksgiving • $$$$*

Mark Picone at Vineland Estates Winery
Local ingredients, subtly prepared, are the stars; Italian flavors add pep. The 1840s farmhouse setting has ambience galore, and a great view of Lake Ontario. ✆ *3620 Moyer Rd, Vineland • Map Q3 • 1 888 846 3526 • $$$$*

Tiara
Savory roast and catch of the day join delights such as lobster agnolotti and lime-crusted rack-of-lamb on the menu of this upscale hotel restaurant. ✆ *155 Byron St, Niagara-on-the-Lake • Map Q3 • 905 468 2195 • $$$$*

The Church
Elegant French food on a seasonal menu, which always includes game. Located in a former church, built in 1874. ✆ *70 Brunswick St, Stratford • Map P2 • 519 273 3424 • Open May–Nov • $$$$*

Bijou
Quirky decor sets the stage for imaginative modern French dishes. ✆ *105 Erie St, Stratford • Map P2 • 519 273 5000 • $$$*

On the Twenty
One of the first Niagara winery restaurants, this charming place favors local ingredients and quality meats. A few pasta dishes. ✆ *3836 Main St, Jordan • Map Q3 • 905 562 7313 • $$$$*

Peller Estates Winery
Enjoy the enchanting vineyard view and the local, seasonal ingredients used in the six- and nine-course tasting menus. ✆ *290 John St E, Niagara-on-the-Lake • Map Q3 • 1 888 673 5537 • $$$$*

Note: *All restaurants accept credit cards and serve vegetarian meals unless otherwise stated*

→

Left **Prince of Wales Hotel** Right **Jakobstettel Inn**

🔟 Country Stays

1 Prince of Wales Hotel
Impeccable service, opulently decorated rooms, a spa, and a wine list to match the fabulous cuisine at this historic hotel in the heart of town. ✎ *6 Picton St, Niagara-on-the-Lake • Map Q3 • 1 888 669 5566 • www.vintageinns.com • $$$$$*

2 Langdon Hall Country House Hotel & Spa
This country mansion welcomes guests with lovingly tended gardens, well-appointed rooms, a spa, and fine cuisine. ✎ *1 Langdon Dr, RR 3, Cambridge • Map P2 • 1 800 268 1898 • www.langdonhall.ca • $$$$$*

3 The Little Inn at Bayfield
This historic inn near Lake Huron, first opened in the 1930s as a coach house, justifiably prides itself on its fine restaurant. Country antiques decorate the rooms. Spa. ✎ *Main St, Bayfield • Map N2 • 1 800 565 1832 • www.littleinn.com • $$$$*

4 Hockley Valley Resort
Nestled in a valley, this is a perfect base for pursuing outdoor activities such as downhill or cross-country skiing, golfing, tennis, and hiking. Spa. ✎ *RR 1, Orangeville • Map P2 • 519 942 0754 • www.hockley.com • $$$$*

5 The Inn at Manitou
This resort, by a pristine Muskoka lake offers swimming, boating, tennis, golf, and more. A team of French chefs prepare fine cuisine. ✎ *McKellar • Map P1 • 1 800 571 8818 • www.manitou-online.com • $$$$*

6 Inn on the Twenty
A luxurious inn in the heart of Niagara wine country renowned for its excellent restaurant *(see p101)*. Spa and winery. ✎ *3845 Main St, Jordan • Map Q3 • 1 800 701 8074 • www.innonthetwenty.com • $$$$*

7 Deerhurst Resort
This lakeside resort set on 800 acres (325 ha) of Muskoka countryside, is suitable for both family vacations and quiet getaways. Spa. ✎ *1235 Deerhurst Dr, Huntsville • Map Q1 • 1 800 461 4393 • www.deerhurstresort.com • $$$$*

8 Jakobstettel
The lovely, relaxing grounds of this Victorian mansion include an outdoor swimming pool. Shopping in St. Jacobs is just a short walk away. ✎ *16 Isabella St, St. Jacobs • Map P2 • 1 800 431 3035 • www.jakobstettel.com • $$$*

9 The Oban Inn
Overlooking Lake Ontario and surrounded by lush gardens, this inn has beautiful rooms and an excellent restaurant. Short walk to the town center. ✎ *160 Front St, Niagara-on-the-Lake • Map Q3 • 1 888 669 5566 • www.vintageinns.com • $$$$*

10 Benmiller Inn
Close to the sandy beaches of Lake Huron, this inn combines country charm and sophisticated elegance. Many of the rooms are in an historic wool mill. Spa. ✎ *RR 4, Goderich • Map N2 • 1 800 265 17111 • www.benmiller.on.ca • $$$$*

For hotel price ranges **See p115**. For more hotels, visit the website www.ontariotravel.net

Left **Handmade straw brooms, St. Jacobs** Right **Jams made from Niagara Peninsula fruits**

Shopping

1 Farmers' Markets
From June to October, usually on Saturday mornings, local farmers sell fresh produce – fiddleheads, white asparagus, wild blueberries and mushrooms, and much more – at over 120 markets throughout Ontario.
🖱 www.farmersmarketsontario.com

2 Quilts
The best place to buy these durable and gorgeous covers is St. Jacobs, where local Mennonite women still practice the traditional craft of hand-quilting. Be sure to stop in at Grey Fort Quilts.
🖱 Grey Fort Quilts: 1425 King St N, St. Jacobs • Map P2 • 1 800 505 2660

3 Fruits and Preserves
In summer and fall, roadside stands in the Niagara region sell luscious fruits. Local companies turn these fruits into delicious jams, which are available at select stores. Greaves preserves are especially popular. 🖱 Greaves Jams and Marmalades: 55 Queen St, Niagara-on-the-Lake • Map Q3 • 1 800 515 9939

4 Handmade Furniture
In southern Ontario, especially around Kitchener-Waterloo, Mennonite men craft durable country-style furniture from local woods such as maple and pine. Watch for signs on the smaller roads pointing the way to local carpenters or head to St. Jacobs Furnishings, a large retail outlet.
🖱 St. Jacobs Furnishings: 878 Weber St N, St. Jacobs • Map P2 • 519 747 1832

5 Factory Outlets
Snap up bargains on brands such as Guess, Nine West, and Nike at Niagara Falls' outlet stores, all under one roof, at Canada One.
🖱 Canada One: 7500 Lundy's Lane, Niagara Falls • Map Q3 • 905 357 2307

6 Maple Syrup
The sap of Ontario's sugar maples is made into delicious pancake syrup and candies, sold at farmers' markets and shops.

7 Arts and Crafts
The work of Ontario's vibrant arts and crafts community, such as pottery, hand-blown glass, and jewelry, can be found thoughout the province at fairs, markets, boutiques, and galleries.

8 Antiques
Hunting for vintage Canadian furniture, toys, silver, and china in the towns of Ontario is great sport. For a large choice of shops, head to Jordan, St. Jacobs, Erin, Neustadt, and Elora.

9 Craft-Brewed Beer
Ontario's microbreweries have enjoyed great popularity in recent years. Many, such as Neustadt Springs, offer tastings and tours.
🖱 Neustadt Springs: 456 Jacob St, Neustadt • Map P2 • 519 799 5790

10 Ontario Wines
Sample award-winning wines at vineyards throughout the Niagara Peninsula before stocking up for the home cellar *(see p100)*.

STREETSMART

TORONTO'S TOP 10

Left **Yorkville Park** Right **Nathan Phillips Square, City Hall**

₁₀ Planning Your Trip

1 When to Go
May through October is Toronto's peak tourist season, but the city is a year-round tourist destination. If you like mild, warm weather, visit in spring or early fall. Summer, especially August, is usually hot and humid. In late fall, the temperature drops as the days shorten. Winter months are cold and snowy, suitable for outdoor activities such as skating and indoor pleasures such as theater and shopping. Accommodation rates are lower at this time.

2 What to Pack
Pack a warm sweater and a light jacket in late spring and early fall. In late fall and early spring, pack a heavier jacket or coat and two warm sweaters. In summer, bring a light sweater or blazer, cotton or linen dresses and slacks, and shorts and T-shirts. Sunglasses and sunscreen are a must, as is an umbrella. In winter, pack a hat, scarf, gloves, and warm coat and waterproof boots.

3 Health Insurance
Unless your health insurance covers medical costs while traveling, buying comprehensive health and dental insurance is strongly recommended: Canada does not provide medical services to visitors free of charge. Many credit card companies provide some degree of insurance; it is worthwhile to check this out before your trip.

4 Passports & Visa
A valid travel document, usually a passport, combined with a visa when needed, must be presented by visitors upon entry to Canada. Residents of many countries, such as the US, Australia, Ireland, New Zealand, and the majority of European countries, including Britain, do not need a visa to visit Canada. Visitors may remain in Canada for up to six months.

5 Customs
Canada's rules governing what can be brought into the country are complex. In general, do not bring live animals, fresh fruit, vegetables, meat, dairy products, plants, or firearms into Canada without first obtaining authorization. Limited amounts of alcohol and tobacco may be imported duty-free by visitors who are of age (19 and 18 years old, respectively). Upon entry into Canada, you must declare any cash amount equal to or over Can$10,000.

6 Driver's License
A driver's license valid in your own country is valid in Ontario for 60 days after you arrive. If you plan to stay longer, an International Driving Permit (obtained in your home country), combined with your license, will allow you to drive in Ontario for up to a year.

7 Car Insurance
Insurance coverage for drivers is mandatory in Ontario; before leaving home, check your own policy to see if you are covered in a rental car. Most rental agencies offer damage and liability insurance; it is a good idea to have both.

8 Electricity
Canada uses a 110-volt, 60-cycle electrical system. Electrical sockets accept two- or three-pronged plugs. Bring a plug adapter and a voltage transformer to run appliances and cell-phone chargers that are not manufactured in North America or that don't have an optional voltage switch.

9 Time Zone
Toronto is in the Eastern Standard Time zone (five hours behind Greenwich Mean Time). Daylight Savings Time begins in early April (clocks are turned forward one hour) and ends in late October (clocks are turned back one hour).

10 Discounts
Most movie theaters, major attractions, and public transit offer reduced rates for people over age 65. Students are eligible for many discounts with ID. Hotels also offer discounts (see p113).

Contact the Canadian embassy or High Commission nearest you for entry requirements, or visit www.cic.gc.ca/english/visit

Left **Sculpture Pearson International Airport** Right **Toronto-to-Rochester ferry**

🔟 Arriving in Toronto

1 Pearson International Airport
Terminal 1 services Air Canada and Air Canada Jazz domestic and inter-national flights, and most Star Alliance airlines operating non-US interna-tional flights. Most other long-haul flights use Terminal 3, as do charter airlines. A train connects terminals 1, 3, and a long-stay parking lot.
✆ *Flight information: Terminal 1: 416 247 7678; Terminal 3: 416 776 5100*

2 Immigration
Cards to be filled out for immigration and customs are distributed during international flights. Only one card need be filled out per family. The immigration officer will ask to see your passport or identifi-cation papers and may pose additional questions.

3 Connections from Pearson Airport
The airport is 16 miles (27 km) northwest of downtown Toronto. The trip takes between 20 and 45 minutes, depending on traffic. Taxis (meter) and limousines (flat rate) at the airport are plentiful. An Airport Express bus leaves for the downtown bus station and several major downtown hotels from the arrivals level of all terminals. If renting a car at the airport and driving downtown, take

Hwy 427 south to the Gardiner Expressway, then drive east toward the city center, alterna-tively, take Hwy 409 east to Hwy 27 southbound, which leads to Hwy 427.
✆ *Airport Express: 1 800 387 6787*

4 Toronto City Centre Airport
This small airport, located by Toronto Harbour and close to downtown, ser-vices short-haul commuter flights to Montreal, Quebec, Ottawa, and Georgian Bay, among other destinations.
✆ *www.torontoport.com*

5 Car Rental
Most car rental companies have booths at Pearson Airport in addi-tion to locations down-town. National, Alamo, and Hertz have booths at Union Station (see p66). For the best rates, book your car in advance. Your hotel can also arrange car rental. To rent a car you will need a valid credit card and driver's license.

6 Public Transit
TTC's (Toronto Transit Commission) Airport Rocket (route number 192) provides service to all Pearson Airport terminals. For downtown destinations, ask the driver for a transfer when boarding. Switch at Kipling Station to the Bloor-Danforth subway.
✆ *www.ttc.ca*

7 Long-Distance Buses
Buses arrive from US and Canada locales at the central bus terminal at 610 Bay St, just north of Dundas. ✆ *Greyhound Canada: 416 367 8747*

8 By Train
Union Station (see p66) is where Amtrak trains arrive from the US and VIA Rail trains pull in from other points in Canada. The train station connects to the Union station stop on the north-south subway line; taxis are readily available out-side the station. Several major hotels are nearby.

9 By Boat or Ferry
Several marinas with excellent facilities provide berth space for practically every type of sea-faring vessel. A new internat-ional ferry terminal is being built off Cherry Street, from where pas-senger and car ferries will head to Rochester, New York. ✆ *Ontario Marinas: 1 888 547 6662; www.marinasontario.com*

10 By Car
Highways leading into Toronto are the 401, just north of the city and bring-ing traffic in from the west and east; the Don Valley Parkway and Hwy 427, running north-south; and the Gardiner Expressway and the Queensway, along Lake Ontario to the south of the city, bringing traffic in from the southwest.

With a few exceptions, you must be over 21 years old to rent a car in Ontario, and some companies do not rent to those under 25

Streetsmart

Streetsmart

Left **Taxi** Right **Boat tour boarding point, Queen's Quay**

🔟 Getting Around Toronto

1 Subway
Toronto's clean and efficient subways are a good way to get around the city. Free route maps are available at all stations. If you are changing subway lines or to a bus or streetcar, take a transfer from one of the red dispensers after paying the fare. Transfers are valid for a one-way continuous trip. ⊗ *6am–1:30am Mon–Sat • 9am–1am Sun*

2 Buses & Streetcars
Bus and streetcar routes crisscross the city and are well-serviced. Make sure to take a transfer from the driver. You will need it to switch to another route or to the subway, and to provide proof of payment if asked.

3 TTC Fares
A ticket or token (coin-like tickets), available in quantities of 5 or 10 at TTC (Toronto Transit Commission) stations and shops displaying a "Ticket Agent" sign, is cheaper than a cash fare. Bus and streetcar drivers don't sell tickets or provide change. It may be worth buying a day pass, sold at subway stations.

4 Wheel-Trans
The TTC operates a door-to-door transit service within the City of Toronto for customers in wheelchairs. ⊗ *Wheel-Trans info: 416 393 4111; to reserve: 416 393 4222*

5 Taxis
Flagging a cab on main downtown streets or at the airport is easy – taxis are plentiful in Toronto. Rates are set by the city. You can also order a cab over the telephone. ⊗ *Beck: 416 751 5555; Co-op: 416 504 2667; Crown Taxi: 416 750 7878; Diamond: 416 366 6868; Yellow Cab: 416 504 4141*

6 Ferries
Ferries to the Toronto Islands depart regularly from the foot of Bay Street, just behind Westin Harbour Castle Hotel. The trip is about 10 minutes. Off-season, all ferries carry bicycles for a small extra fee. In summer, the Centre Island ferry doesn't *(see p14)*. ⊗ *Ferry schedules: 416 392 8193*

7 Walking
By foot is the best way to explore Toronto neighborhoods. Central downtown Toronto streets are fairly safe, even at night, but if in doubt check with your concierge. In winter, escape the cold by going underground to the PATH system *(see p25)*.

8 Cycling
Cyclists must follow the same rules of the road as drivers. Some streets have cycling lanes but most don't. Maps of cycling lanes and paths are available online or at City Hall. The Martin Goodman Trail *(see p94)* is a good alternative to busy streets. Bike theft is a concern in the city; lock up your bike securely when not in use. In general, bikes may not be ridden on sidewalks, and while wearing a helmet is not mandatory, it is always a good idea to do so: streetcar tracks in particular are a hazard to cyclists. Bikes are allowed on most TTC buses and subways during non-peak hours. ⊗ *www.city.toronto.on.ca/cycling*

9 Driving
The grid system of Toronto's streets makes driving easy, but a good map is still essential: many streets are one-way. Most major two-way streets forbid left-hand turns during rush hours. Highways are busy during rush hours – especially Hwy 401, Hwy 427, and the Gardiner Expressway – and are best avoided. It is illegal to pass a streetcar on the right-hand side when it is stopped to let passengers on or off. Wait 6.5 ft (2 m) behind the rear doors until all the doors have closed. Before opening the car door or making a right-hand turn, double-check for cyclists.

10 Boat Tours
Several companies offer hour-long tours of Toronto Harbour. You can also book a day tour on a three-masted schooner. All depart from Queen's Quay docks *(see p62)*. ⊗ *www.torontoharbour.com*

Left **Cyclists along the lakefront** Right **Streetcars on Dundas Street**

🔟 Toronto on a Budget

1 Free Entertainment
Free entertainment is to be had year-round in Toronto. From Winterfest to Pride Week to dragon boat races, there's an event for everyone *(see pp46–7)*. Throughout the summer, a multitude of free events are held at Harbourfront *(see p63)*, and in late June and early July, jazz festivals keep the fans busy downtown and in The Beach *(see p47)*. There are free celebratory concerts and fireworks on July 1 (Canada Day) and New Year's Eve. In January, bands perform at Nathan Phillips Square during WinterCity *(see p47)*. 🖎 www.city.toronto.on.ca/events; www.torontowide.com

2 Parks and Beaches
Whether your taste leans toward roller-blading, walking, playing ball, or simply sunning yourself on the sand, Toronto's parks and beaches *(see pp40–41)* offer many great ways to relax. Several have excellent sports facilities, as well as grills and picnic tables. 🖎 www.city.toronto.on.ca/parks

3 Cheap Eats
While you can eat fairly cheaply at fast-food chains such as the home-grown Tim Hortons, ethnic restaurants are an excellent alternative. The range of cuisines is astonishing, the prices reasonable *(see p81)*.

4 Free Art
Clustered in Yorkville *(see p59)* around Hazelton Lane and Cumberland Street, on West Queen Street West *(see p58)*, and at 25 Morrow Avenue near the Roncesvalles neighborhood *(see p39)* are galleries selling works by local and international artists. Entry to some public and corporate galleries *(see pp34–5)* is free. The outdoor public art is also worth checking out *(see p37)*.

5 Free Tours
Heritage Toronto gives free walking tours in summer, covering such diverse topics as the city's railroad history or its water supply. Book ahead or just show up. 🖎 416 338 0684 • mid-Jun–mid-Oct • www.heritagetoronto.org

6 Package Deals
The City of Toronto offers packages for short stays by US and Canadian visitors throughout the year to promote hotels, restaurants, and attractions. A package typically includes a one-night hotel stay, three-course meal, show, and breakfast, but there are several options, varying from month to month. 🖎 www.torontotourism.com

7 CityPass
This pass is available online and payable in US dollars or in Canadian funds at the ticket booth of the attractions featured: Casa Loma *(see pp18–19)*, CN Tower *(see pp12–13)*, Art Gallery of Ontario *(see pp16–17)*, Royal Ontario Museum *(see pp8–11)*, Ontario Science Centre *(see p34)*, and Toronto Zoo *(see p91)*. CityPass offers substantial discounts on admission – amounting to 50 percent if you visit all participating sights. It is valid for nine days from your first sight visit. 🖎 www.citypass.com

8 Transit Savings
Single day passes, valid weekdays, are available at all subway stations; group passes for two or more are valid Sundays and public holidays. Both offer real savings. Monthly passes and passes for convention visitors are also available. 🖎 416 393 4636 • www.ttc.ca

9 Free Admission Days
Some city attractions, such as the Royal Ontario Museum *(see pp8–11)* and Art Gallery of Ontario *(see pp16–17)*, offer one free day or evening per week. Bear in mind that although cheaper, the crowds can be greater.

10 Hotel Savings
Many hotels offer discounts when booked online. If booking directly or through an agent, ask about discounts. Members of auto clubs and AARP (American Association of Retired Persons) often qualify for discounts.

Harbourfront hosts free concerts, readings, festivals, and more year-round; visit its website at www.harbourfrontcentre.com

109

Left **Telephone booth sign** Center **Tix ticket center sign** Right **Wheelchair access sign**

🔟 Useful Information

1 Drinking
The legal drinking age in Ontario is 19. Ontario has strict laws about drinking in public: open bottles of alcohol are not allowed in public places. Fenced-off areas are set aside for selling and consuming alcohol at large events.

2 Media
The two largest Canadian newspapers are produced in Toronto: The *Globe and Mail* and the *Toronto Star*, along with a daily tabloid, *Toronto Sun*. Popular radio stations include CBC Radio One (FM 99.1) for news, CBC Radio Two (FM 92.1) for classical music, Jazz Channel Plus (FM 91.1) for jazz, CHFI (FM 98.1) for easy-listening music, CHUM (FM 104.5) and CILQ (FM 107.5) for rock music. The most popular Canadian TV stations are CBC, CTV, GLOBAL, BRAVO and CityTV and, in Ontario, TVO.

3 Entertainment Listings
Toronto weeklies *Now* and *Eye* are available free at cafés, bars, bookshops, libraries, and street boxes throughout the city and are the best sources for checking the happenings in the local music and art scene. The monthly magazine *Toronto Life* is also helpful. These listings are also online. ❧ www.eye. net • www.now.com • www.torontolife.com

4 Currency
The Canadian unit of currency is the dollar, which is divided into 100 cents. Coins come in denominations of 1, 5, 10, and 25 cents, and 1 and 2 dollars. Bank notes (bills) come in denominations of $5, $10, $20, $50, $100, and $500. Plan to arrive with at least $50 to $100 in local currency and acquire change as soon as you can for tipping and transit.

5 Taxes
In Canada, taxes are not included in the listed price unless specified, so when making a purchase reckon with a further 8 percent for PST (provincial sales tax) and 7 percent for GST (goods and services tax). Some taxes are refundable when you leave Canada *(see p112)*.

6 Websites
Extensive information on the city of Toronto and the province of Ontario is available on the internet. ❧ www.toronto.ca • www.ontariotravel.net • www.ontournet.com

7 Telephones
Public telephones are often both coin and card operated. Local calls cost $0.50; directory assistance (411) is free. Post offices, most convenience stores, and specially marked Bell machines sell phone cards. Within Toronto you must prefix the local telephone number with the area code 416, or with 905 for calls to Greater Toronto. For a long-distance number in North America, dial the prefix 1 and then the city code. To dial abroad, dial 011 + country code + city code (dropping any 0).

8 Public Holidays
New Year's Day (Jan 1), Good Friday and Easter Monday (Mar or Apr), Victoria Day (usually 3rd Mon in May), Canada Day (Jul 1), civic holiday (1st Mon in Aug), Labour Day (1st Mon in Sep), Thanksgiving (2nd Mon in Oct), Christmas Day (Dec 25), Boxing Day (Dec 26). Remembrance Day (Nov 11) is a holiday for banks and government offices.

9 Disabled Visitors
Bathrooms in many establishments in older buildings are located up or down a flight of stairs and are not easily accessible; large entertainment venues. Toronto's streetcars are not wheelchair accessible, but lift buses designed for people with mobility aids run on many routes, and 10 subway stations have elevators. Transit on the free city Wheel-Trans can be reserved, but you must register first *(see p108)*.

10 Consulates
In emergencies, your consulate may give assistance. ❧ UK: 77 Bay St, Map K3, 416 593 1267 • US: 360 University Ave, Map K2, 416 595 1700

For information on transit for the physically disabled, visit the website www.city.toronto.on.ca/ttc/accessible.htm

Left **Hospital sign** Center **Police car** Right **No smoking sign**

🔟 Security & Health

1 Theft Prevention
Pickpockets are present in all large cities, especially in crowded places. Pay attention to your surroundings and avoid being distracted, especially if someone bumps into you. Don't carry more cash with you than you need and don't carry your wallet in a back pocket. If you have a purse, ensure it closes tightly. Always watch your luggage carefully at airports, at bus and train stations, and when checking in and out of your hotel. Leave valuables in the hotel's safe.

2 Hotel Room Safety
When you've checked into your room, look on the back of the entrance door for a map showing the escape route to take in case of fire. Always leave the security latch in place when in your room and don't admit strangers. Some hotels have floors for women-only – ask when booking, if you are a woman traveling alone.

3 Food Safety
Any establishment in Toronto that serves food, including pubs and delicatessens, are inspected regularly by city health officials. The green, yellow, or red card hanging in the window reflects the overall mark given on conditions such as cleanliness. Green denotes a full pass, yellow a conditional pass, red a failure.

4 Telephone Helplines
Various helplines are available to call in a crisis.
🌐 Emergency: 911
• Toronto Police Services: 416 808 2222 • Kids Help Phone: 1 800 668 6868
• Assaulted Women's Help Line: 416 863 0511
• Distress Centre of Toronto: 416 408 4357
• Poison Control: 416 813 5900 • Telehealth Ontario: 1 866 797 0000

5 Public Transit
Always look to your right to make sure no cars are coming before exiting a streetcar. Subway platforms provide designated waiting areas; these are recommended at night. Available on TTC buses, Request Stop allows a woman to get off a bus at locations between regular TTC stops. Tell the driver at least one stop ahead of where you want to get off and leave the bus by the front doors. The rear doors will remain closed so that no one can follow you off.

6 Knowing Your Surroundings
Avoid dark places at night, especially if you are on your own. Carry a good map with you and check out the route to and from your destination before starting out. If you plan on returning late, make sure you have enough change and cash to call for and pay for a taxi.

7 Hospital Emergency Rooms
Emergency treatment is available 24 hours a day.
🌐 st Michael's: 30 Bond St, Map L3, 416 360 4000
• Toronto General: 200 Elizabeth St, Map K2, 416 340 3946 • Mt Sinai: 600 University Ave, Map K2, 416 586 5054 • Hospital for Sick Children: 555 University Ave, Map K2, 416 813 1500 • Toronto East General: 825 Coxwell St, Map B2, 416 461 8272

8 Dental Emergencies
An emergency referral service, the Academy of Dentistry, links you with a nearby dentist after regular office hours. After midnight, go to a hospital emergency room. 🌐 Academy of Dentistry: 416 967 5649

9 Smoking
Toronto is a smoke-free city except in designated smoking rooms at some bars, clubs, restaurants, and in some workplaces. All public spaces are smoke-free.

10 Pharmacies
There are hundreds of pharmacies in Toronto. The majority are open from 9am to 9 or 10pm and many are open until later. Five 24-hour Shoppers Drug Mart pharmacies serve the city. The most central is on Bay Street.
🌐 Shoppers Drug Mart: 700 Bay St, Map K2, 416 979 2424 or 1 800 746 7737

Check with your cellphone provider before leaving home to find out if your cellphone is serviced in Canada

Left **The Colonnade, Bloor Street West** Right **Vintage clothing store, Kensington Market**

⑩ Shopping Tips

① Store Hours
Most shops are open 10am to 6pm, Monday to Saturday (often later on Thursday). Department stores and shops in malls and commercial districts may keep longer hours, from 10am to 9pm, Monday to Saturday, and from noon to 5pm on Sunday. Widely observed retail holidays are Christmas, January 1, July 1, Labour Day, and Thanksgiving.

② Payment
MasterCard, American Express, and Visa credit cards are widely accepted, Diner's Club and Discovery less so. Bank debit cards compatible with the Interac, Plus, or Cirrus systems are also widely accepted. You will need your PIN.

③ Sales & Returns
Look for end-of-season savings on merchandise. Excellent savings are to be had on Boxing Day (December 26), when prices at many stores are reduced dramatically. Discounted items (and sometimes even those at full price) may not be returnable, or may be exchanged only, and within a certain time period. Be sure to ask about the return policy before making a purchase.

④ Department Stores
Toronto's two department store chains, The Bay (see p25) and Sears, carry practically everything. The smaller Holt Renfrew (see p77) sells high-end clothing and accessories.
🛇 Sears: Eaton Centre, 1 Dundas St W • Map L3

⑤ Shopping Malls
The largest downtown mall is Eaton Centre (see pp24–5). Other malls are Queen's Quay Terminal (see p63), Hazelton Lanes (see p77), Manulife Centre (see p77), College Park, and the network of malls on the PATH system (see p25). 🛇 College Park: 444 Yonge St • Map L2

⑥ Music
Music giant HMV has a huge selection. For local flavor and good prices, visit Sam the Record Man (see p78). Classical and jazz lovers should head to L'Atelier Grigorian. For vinyl, try Kops Records. 🛇 L'Atelier Grigorian: 70 Yorkville Ave, Map C3 • HMV: 333 Yonge St, Map L2 • Kops Records: 229 Queen St W, Map J4

⑦ Books
Chapters, Indigo, and BookCity have good selections and many locations. Other excellent bookshops are Nicolas Hoare for architecture and art, Open Air Books & Maps for maps and travel guides, Pages Books & Magazines for contemporary literature, and Bakka-Phoenix Books for science fiction. 🛇 Bakka-Phoenix Books: 598 Yonge St, Map L1 • Book City: 501 Bloor St W, Map B3 • Chapters: 110 Bloor St W, Map C3 • Indigo: 55 Bloor St W, Map D3 • Nicolas Hoare: 45 Front St E, Map L5 • Open Air Books & Maps: 25 Toronto St, Map L4 • Pages Books & Magazines: 256 Queen St W, Map L2

⑧ Alcohol
Sales of alcohol are restricted to LCBO (Liquor Control Board of Ontario) outlets (wine, spirits, and beer), the Beer Store (beer and coolers), and the Wine Rack (selected Ontario wines). 🛇 www.lcbo.com, 1 800 668 5226 • www.thebeerstore.ca • Wine Rack, 905 564 6900

⑨ Convenience Stores
Small shops selling cigarettes, toiletry necessities, cold drinks, snacks and fresh produce, and lottery tickets are ubiquitous in Toronto. Many also sell transit tickets.

⑩ Tax Refunds
Books and groceries are exempt from the 8 percent PST (provincial sales tax), but most other items are subject to up to 15 percent sales tax (see p110). International visitors who have spent over $200 are entitled to a refund of the 7 percent GST (goods and services tax) within 60 days of purchase, excluding GST levied on restaurant meals, drinks, tobacco, and transport. Save your receipts. 🛇 Visitor Rebate Program: 1 800 668 4748

The shopping malls Queen's Quay Terminal **See p63** and Eaton Centre **See pp24–5** are open on public holidays

Left **Hot dog cart** Right **Entrance, Royal Meridien King Edward Hotel**

ＴＯＰ10 Accommodation & Dining Tips

1 Hotel Taxes
In Ontario, accommodation is taxed with a 5 percent accommodation tax and a 7 percent GST (goods and services tax). An additional 3 percent destination tax is also levied on hotel rooms in the City of Toronto. You are entitled to a refund of the GST for hotel accommodation for short stays.

2 Rooms
In general, hotel rooms are well furnished and of a fairly good size. Most have two double beds or one queen- or king-sized bed; standard twin-bedded rooms may also be available. If you are sensitive to noise, ask for a room away from the elevator and the ice and dispensing machines; if sensitive to smoke, ask for a smoke-free room.

3 Rack Rates
Hotel rates vary according to the hotel category, and the time of week and season. Peak rates are weekdays and from April to December. Rack rates, the basic room rates, are the ones used in this book to provide a guide price. It is almost always possible to get a better deal, especially if you book online. And too, discounts are often available to members of clubs such as automobile associations or the Elderhostel. When booking, ask what special rates apply and make sure to bring proof of membership with you (see p109).

4 Concierges
Mid- and large-size hotels have concierges on staff whose job it is to cater to the needs and whims of the guests. They will procure tickets to shows and sports games, make restaurant reservations, arrange transportation, and offer helpful tips.

5 Extra Costs
Parking at downtown hotels is almost always extra, paid on a per-night basis. Telephone calls made from your in-room phone can be expensive, as can drinks and snacks consumed from the room's minibar. Beware: These costs can add up quickly, and will appear on your final room bill.

6 Restaurant Reservations
Most restaurants take reservations and it is a good idea to book a table at a popular dining spot well in advance of your trip. Mention if you have special needs or dietary requirements. It is considered good form to cancel your reservation if your plans change.

7 Tipping
Tips and service charges are not usually added to dining bills. For service at restaurants, cafés, and clubs, plan on tipping about 15 percent of the pre-tax amount. An easy way of estimating the tip is to add up the taxes on the bill. At bars, leave a dollar or two for the bartender. Tip porters and bellhops at least $1 per bag or suitcase; cloakroom attendants, $1 per garment; and chambermaids, a minimum of $1 to $2 per day. A hotel doorman will also appreciate a dollar or two for his services.

8 Dress Codes
Jacket and tie are almost never required in restaurants, though many diners opt to wear them on a special evening out, especially to an upscale place. Some clubs, however, may not allow you in if you are wearing sneakers or jeans.

9 Cellphones
At most restaurants, it is considered uncourteous to leave your cellphone turned on or to carry on cellphone conversations inside.

10 Meal Times
Breakfast is usually served in diners and coffee shops from about 6am to 10am. Lunch is available from about 11:30am to 2pm, dinner between about 5pm and 10pm. Many restaurants and pubs offer a late-night menu. Brunches are often served on weekends only – and at some spots, on Sundays only – usually from 11am–2pm or later.

Left **Lobby, Selby Hotel** Right **Suite, Roehampton Hotel**

🔟 Inexpensive Hotels

1 Casa Loma Inn
This stately home dating to 1894 is now a charming inn. Each of the 23 rooms – and all are unique – have a fridge, microwave, and coffee-maker. Some rooms have fireplaces. There is no elevator serving the inn's three floors. ✆ 21 Walmer Rd • Map C2 • 416 924 4540 • $$

2 Hotel Victoria
Just steps from Union Station in the city's Financial District, this small hotel, with just 56 rooms, offers all the amenities of a large hotel, along with excellent service. It is close to many top attractions. ✆ 56 Yonge St • Map L4 • 416 363 1666 • www.hotelvictoria-toronto. com • $$$

3 Madison Manor
Featuring many unusual details, including fireplaces and alcove windows, the owners of this lovingly restored Victorian mansion aim to make guests feel as though they have stepped into an English country inn. To further the illusion, there's a pub next door. ✆ 20 Madison Ave • Map C3 • 416 922 5579 • www.madisonavenuepub. com/madisonmanor • $$

4 The Suites at One King West
Located in Toronto's Financial District, this hotel is uniquely built atop an historic 1912 building

that once housed the Dominion Bank of Canada. Opened in 2005, the hotel boasts a 24-hour business center, bistro, and private club. The views are breathtaking. ✆ 1 King St W • Map K4 • 416 548 8101 • www.one kingwest.com • $$$

5 Selby Hotel and Suites
Listed as a historical landmark building by the City, this noble Victorian mansion dates from 1880 and has been a hotel since 1915, hosting guests such as Ernest Hemingway, who resided here in the 1920s. It is now part of the Howard-Johnson chain. The rooms have high ceilings and are comfortably furnished. ✆ 592 Sherbourne St • Map D3 • 416 921 3142 • www.hotelselby.com • $$

6 Travelodge Toronto Downtown West
On King Street just west of Bathurst Street, near top restaurants and clubs, this three-floor motel offers free parking in its courtyard. Rooms are standard but spacious. Breakfast is included. ✆ 621 King St W • Map G4 • 416 504 7441 • www. travelodgetoronto downtown.com • $$

7 The Strathcona Hotel
Guests enjoy the modern, updated rooms (including that rare type – a single), and use of a fitness club

next door. The hotel is right by the Air Canada Centre and close to other major attractions; a pub and restaurant are located in the hotel. ✆ 60 York St • Map K4 • 416 363 3321 • $$

8 Roehampton Hotel and Suites
With its heated rooftop pool and well-appointed rooms and suites, this Best Western is a pleasant, affordable home away from home. It is a short walk to the Eglinton subway station and the many excellent shops and restaurants nearby. ✆ 808 Mt Pleasant Rd • Map B2 • 416 487 5101 • www.best western.com • $$

9 Four Points Sheraton
Facing Lake Ontario, just a few steps away, this small hotel is about a 15-minute drive from downtown. Parking is free, rooms are large and well-furnished, and there's a restaurant and bar. ✆ 1926 Lake Shore Blvd W • Map A2 • 416 766 4392 • www.fourpointstoronto. com • $$$

10 Valhalla Inn
Business travelers as well as families with children are cared for in this modern, multi-story hotel located west of Toronto. Every amenity is offered, including an indoor pool and two restaurants. ✆ 1 Valhalla Inn Rd • Map A2 • 416 239 2391 • www. valhalla-inn.com • $$$

Note: Unless otherwise stated, all hotels accept credit cards and have private bathrooms and air conditioning

Price Categories

For a standard, double room per night (with breakfast if included), taxes and extra charges.

$	under $100
$$	$100–150
$$$	$150–200
$$$$	$200–300
$$$$$	over $300

Above **Pool, Grand Hotel**

🔟 Mid-priced Hotels

1 Holiday Inn on King

Whether you are visiting for business or leisure, this downtown hotel is good value. Heated rooftop pool, in-room spa services, restaurant, bar, and deli. ⚅ *370 King St W • Map J4 • 416 599 4000 • www.hiok.com • $$$$*

2 Novotel Toronto Center

Well-placed near many downtown attractions, this hotel is a good representative of the French chain. The large rooms are functional, and there is a lovely lobby, a fitness room, and indoor pool. ⚅ *45 The Esplanade • Map L5 • 416 367 8900 • www.novotel.com • $$$$*

3 Doubletree International Plaza Hotel Toronto Airport

While the parents attend a conference, kids are kept busy in the indoor waterpark and supervised children's program. This hotel near Pearson Airport has 433 exceptionally well-appointed guestrooms and is a popular conference center. A variety of restaurants and bars ensure you rarely need leave the premises. ⚅ *655 Dixon Rd • Map A2 • 416 244 1711 • www.doubletree.com • $$$*

4 Courtyard Toronto Downtown

An indoor pool, whirlpool, exercise room, and sauna are among the amenities found in this comfortable 17-floor Marriott hotel. With many high-tech conveniences in the rooms, such as high-speed Internet access and phones with data ports, a working stay here is enjoyable. ⚅ *475 Yonge St • Map L2 • 416 924 0611 • www.marriott.com • $$$*

5 Grand Hotel and Suites Toronto

Rooms and suites in this large boutique hotel are spacious and luxuriously furnished; some have private terraces. Features include an opulent pool, a huge rooftop patio with two whirlpools and spectacular city views, a spa and fitness club, a business center, and meeting rooms. ⚅ *225 Jarvis St • Map M3 • 416 863 9000 • www.grandhotel toronto.com • $$$$*

6 Radisson Plaza Hotel Admiral Toronto Harbourfront

Bright, large rooms in this hotel steps from Lake Ontario and harbourfront attractions appeal to both business and leisure travelers. There is a good restaurant, and a rooftop pool and deck overlooking the lake. ⚅ *294 Queens Quay W • Map J6 • 416 203 3333 • www.radisson.com • $$$$*

7 Sheraton Fallsview

East-facing rooms in this comfortable high-rise hotel offer fantastic views of Niagara Falls. Staff is extremely knowledgable and helpful; rooms are large and well-appointed. ⚅ *6755 Fallsview Blvd, Niagara Falls • Map Q3 • 1 800 618 9059 • www.fallsview.com • $$$$*

8 Howard Johnson Hotel – Downtown

This Yorkville hotel with only 69 rooms offers good value and an excellent location, close to top attractions and shopping. Rooms are ample. ⚅ *89 Avenue Rd • Map C3 • 416 964 1220 • www.hojo.com • $$$*

9 The Old Mill Inn

This boutique inn on the Humber River is a 15-minute drive west of downtown. All 47 rooms overlook the river; the 13 suites are located in the historic old mill building. Rooms are luxurious and there's an excellent restaurant, spa, and wellness center. ⚅ *21 Old Mill Rd • Map A2 • 416 236-2641 • www.oldmill toronto.com • $$$$*

10 Cambridge Suites

Excellent service is standard at this hotel offering two-room suites only. Fully equipped work areas have all the bells and whistles, including a fax machine. Microwave, fridge, and coffeemaker are in every suite. ⚅ *15 Richmond St E • Map L4 • 416 368 1990 • www.cambridgesuitestoronto.com • $$$*

For accommodation outside Toronto **See p102**

Streetsmart

Left **The Royal York** Right **Hotel Le Germain**

Luxury & Boutique Hotels

1 Soho Metropolitan
Lovers of luxury adore this boutique hotel in the Entertainment District. Duvets, walk-in closets, extravagant bathrooms with heated marble floors, and many high-tech gadgets are standard. Senses, a top restaurant, is located on the ground floor (see p52). ✆ 318 Wellington St W • Map J4 • 416 599 8800 • www.metropolitan.com/soho • $$$$$

2 Le Royal Meridien King Edward
Opened in 1903, this grand historic hotel, a member of the Leading Hotels in the World, offers elegantly appointed rooms, courteous service, spa, and every possible amenity; guests want for nothing. ✆ 37 King St E • Map L4 • 416 863 9700 • www.lemeridien.com/kingedward • $$$$$

3 Four Seasons
Coddling its guests with every comfort, and in a prime Yorkville location, this hotel is a favorite with celebrities. The excellent Truffles restaurant and chic Avenue bar (see p56) add to the elegance. ✆ 21 Avenue Rd • Map C3 • 416 964 0411 • www.fourseasons.com/toronto • $$$$$

4 Sutton Place Hotel
This modern 33-floor hotel features upscale guestrooms, suites, and apartments, all beautifully appointed with fine antiques and original art. Its restaurant, Accents, offers continental cuisine. ✆ 955 Bay St • Map K1 • 416 924 9221 • www.suttonplace.com • $$$$

5 Park Hyatt Toronto
Luxurious, spacious rooms with marble bathrooms and free high-speed Internet access, attentive service, and a central Yorkville location, make this classy hotel a great favorite. The Roof Lounge (see p56) provides a spectacular view of the city, and its posh Stillwater Spa is one of the city's best. ✆ 4 Avenue Rd • Map C3 • 416 925 1234 • http://park toronto.hyatt.com • $$$$

6 Fairmont Royal York
Across from Union Station, this large hotel has been a Toronto landmark since 1929. The magnificent lobby is a fitting backdrop for the many heads of state who have stayed here. There are several restaurants and bars, including the cozy Library Bar (see p67), and a great spa. ✆ 100 Front St W • Map K5 • 416 368 2511 • www.fairmont.com • $$$$$

7 Hotel le Germain
With its modern, understated decor, this boutique hotel is the very height of elegance. Its mission – to promote relaxation while pampering its guests with luxury – succeeds every time. ✆ 30 Mercer St • Map J4 • 416 345 9500 • www.germaintoronto.com • $$$$$

8 Windsor Arms
Personal service is writ large in this elegant hotel with just 28 guest rooms, located on the first four floors of a 14-story building. Guests enjoy the two-floor spa and delight in the cuisine of Courtyard Café (see p54). There's also a caviar and champagne bar. ✆ 18 Thomas St • Map C3 • 416 971 9666 • www.windsorarmshotel.com • $$$$$

9 The Drake Hotel
A former flophouse has been transformed into a hip, artsy boutique hotel. Rooms, decorated in an eclectic mix of vintage and modern, are small but well-designed to maximize space. The Drake Lounge is bustling on weekends (see p80). ✆ 1150 Queen St W • Map A4 • 416 531 5042 • www.thedrakehotel.ca • $$$$

10 Pantages Suites
Deluxe modern accommodation with nice touches such as a washer and dryer in all rooms, and stunning city views from the windows of this 45-story hotel and condominium tower. ✆ 200 Victoria St • Map L4 • 416 362 1777 • www.pantageshotel.com • $$$$

Above **Lobby, Hilton Hotel**

Price Categories		
For a standard,	**$**	under $100
double room per	**$$**	$100–150
night (with breakfast	**$$$**	$150–200
if included), taxes	**$$$$**	$200–300
and extra charges.	**$$$$$**	over $300

🔟 Business-Friendly Hotels

1 Hilton Toronto
Centrally located in the financial district, this Hilton is geared to businesspeople. Standard rooms are spacious and modern, suites ideal for longer stays, and executive rooms provide extras such as special work chairs. ✪ 145 Richmond St W • Map K4 • 416 869 3456 • www.hilton.com • $$$$

2 Westin Harbour Castle
With a location on Lake Ontario right beside the ferry docks, yet close to downtown, this high-rise hotel offers stunning views from its ample rooms. With its pool, fitness room, and outdoor tennis court, along with spacious meeting rooms and full business service, it feels like a resort smack in the middle of the city. ✪ 1 Harbour Sq • Map K6 • 416 869 1600 • www.westin.com/harbourcastle • $$$$$

3 Toronto Marriott Airport
Convenient to Pearson Airport, 405 rooms in this Marriott are designed for the business traveler. All phones are wired with data ports and rooms have high-speed Internet access. Meeting rooms are plentiful, and an indoor pool and health club help shed the stress. ✪ 901 Dixon Rd • Map A2 • 416 674 9400 • www.marriott.com • $$$$$

4 Sheraton Centre
Steps from City Hall, this hotel complex bustles year-round with conventioneers and tour groups. Akin to a small city – there are 1,377 rooms – efficient service keeps the wheels turning smoothly and the guests content. ✪ 123 Queen St W • Map K4 • 416 361 1000 • www.sheraton toronto.com • $$$$$

5 InterContinental Toronto Centre
Attached to the Convention Centre, this newly renovated hotel provides attentive service and excellent business facilities. The eighth floor is reserved for Priority Club business guests. ✪ 225 Front St W • Map J5 • 416 597 1400 • www.ichotelsgroup.com • $$$$

6 Delta Chelsea
The biggest hotel in Canada, with 1,590 guest rooms, caters equally well to business travelers and families. An indoor waterslide, daycare center, and more keep the children amused. ✪ 33 Gerrard St W • Map L2 • 416 595 1975 • www.deltahotels.com • $$$

7 Wyndham Bristol Place Toronto
Five minutes from Pearson Airport, the hotel surprises at check-in with a waterfall in its lobby. Guests appreciate the modern, spacious rooms, personalized service, fitness center, indoor pool, and other amenities. ✪ 950 Dixon Rd • Map A2 • 416 675 9444 • www.wyndham.com • $$$

8 Metropolitan Hotel Toronto
Elegant contemporary decor and luxurious touches such as down duvets pamper travelers. Two award-winning restaurants, Hemispheres and Lai Wah Heen (see p53), add to the pleasure of a stay here. ✪ 108 Chestnut St • Map K3 • 416 977 5000 • www.metropolitan.com • $$$$$

9 Toronto Marriott Downtown Eaton Centre
Featuring a full business center with secretarial service, dedicated business guestrooms, and 18 meeting rooms, this 18-story hotel is conveniently located beside the Eaton Centre (see pp24–5). ✪ 525 Bay St • Map K3 • 416 597 9200 • www.marriott.com • $$$$

10 Westin Prince Toronto
Set in a large park northeast of downtown, this hotel is an oasis of comfort. Its several bars and restaurants – including Katsura (see p95) – handsome rooms, and a business center explain this hotel's popularity. ✪ 900 York Mills Rd • Map B1 • 416 444 2511 • www.westin.com/prince • $$$$$

Left **The Red Door** Right **Toronto Townhouse**

Bed & Breakfasts

1 Toronto Townhouse
This is a 140-year-old beautifully renovated and raved-about home in leafy Cabbagetown. It is located close to Riverdale Farm, an area of great shopping, and Yonge subway. ✆ *213 Carlton • Map E3 • 877 500 0466 • www.toronto-townhouse. com • $$$$*

2 Accommodating the Soul
In a lovely 1911 home with a lush English-style garden, this B&B in The Beach and a short walk from Ashbridges Bay, rents out three antiques-furnished rooms to guests. A delicious hot breakfast is served in your choice of the garden or dining room. ✆ *114 Waverley Rd • Map B2 • 416 686 0619 • $$*

3 Albert's Inn
Four cozy rooms in a Victorian house decorated to the nines with all things British, from antiques to bric-a-brac, offer an unforgettably eccentric stay in Cabbagetown. Alfred Pimblett, the owner, amuses guests with take-offs on the Queen of England. ✆ *242 Gerrard St E • Map E4 • 416 921 6898 • www.pimblett.ca • $$*

4 Toronto Island
On Ward's Island in Toronto Harbour, this cottage B&B, in the oldest building on the island, (1882), is just a 10-minute ferry ride from downtown, but it feels like a world away. Available year-round, the two rooms share a kitchenette. Use of bicycles is free, dinner is served off-season upon request, and, in winter, there's cross-country skiing. ✆ *8 Lakeshore Ave, Ward's Island • Map E6 • 416 203 0935 • $*

5 Ainsley House
Located in the upscale Rosedale area, minutes from great shopping and some of the city's best-known attractions, three well-appointed guest rooms in a charming older home beckon. ✆ *19 Elm Ave • Map D3 • 1 888 423 3337 • www. ainsleyhouse.com • $*

6 The Mulberry Tree
Elegant details original to this 1901 home, such as fine oak floors and high ceilings, add to the charm of this downtown property. There's a small guest lounge. The attentive, friendly hosts keep the cookie jar filled and provide business facilities for guests if needed. ✆ *122 Isabella St • Map D3 • 416 960 5249 • $$*

7 Au Petit Paris
Just east of downtown and within a 15-minute walk of the upscale shops on Bloor Street and in Yorkville, this B&B has a Paris flair. Its four rooms, all with private baths, are decorated in shades of ochre and red. Breakfast is served in the dining room or on the rooftop patio. ✆ *3 Selby St • Map D3 • 416 928 1348 • $$*

8 The Red Door
Located near the beautiful High Park and Roncesvalles neighborhood, this gorgeous home, set on a quiet residential street, has three spacious, well-lit rooms – all with private bathrooms – delicious gourmet breakfasts, and off-street parking for visitors. ✆ *301 Indian Rd • Map A2 • 416 604 0544 • $$$*

9 The French Connection
Stylish quarters within walking distance of Casa Loma and several fine restaurants, this B&B has six rooms (three with private bath), an elegant living room with grand piano, and a lovely garden. ✆ *102 Burnside Dr • 416 537 7741 • $$$*

10 House on McGill
Six tastefully decorated rooms, some with shared baths, and reasonable prices make this B&B in a restored Victorian townhouse a good choice for the budget-conscious traveler. It is centrally located, about a 10-minute walk from the Eaton Centre. ✆ *110 McGill St • Map L2 • 416 351 1503 • $$*

For more bed & breakfasts, visit the websites www.bbtoronto.com, for Toronto, and www.fobba.com, for Ontario

Price Categories

For a standard, double room per night (with breakfast if included), taxes and extra charges.	$	under $100
	$$	$100–150
	$$$	$150–200
	$$$$	$200–300
	$$$$$	over $300

Above **Global Village Backpacker's Hostel**

Budget Accommodation

1 Annex Quest House

With its dark pine furnishings, natural decor, vibrant colors, and tastefully appointed guest rooms dedicated to one of the four elements – earth, fire, air, and water – travelers will enjoy the calming atmosphere of this retreat from the city. Located near Casa Loma. ✆ *83 Spadina Rd • Map C2 • 416 922 1934 • www.annexquesthouse. com • $*

2 Quality Hotel & Suites Airport East

In the west of the city, near Pearson Airport and major traffic arteries, this hotel has large, comfortable standard rooms and suites. Extra features include free parking and airport shuttle service running from 3am to 11pm. ✆ *2180 Islington Ave • Map A2 • 416 240 9090 • $*

3 Victoria University

Located on the University of Toronto campus, Victoria University opens its doors to budget-minded travelers during summer-semester holidays, mid-May to the end of August. A quiet setting combined with a central location make these lodgings an excellent base from which to explore the city. ✆ *73 Queen's Park Crescent E • Map K1 • 416 585 4524 • www.vicu.utoronto.ca • $*

4 Neill-Wycik College Hotel

This student residence turns into a guest house from early May to the end of August. While the rooms are spartan and bathrooms are shared, the price is right for tight budgets. Groups are welcome. The central location means many of the city's top destinations are in walking distance. ✆ *96 Gerrard St E • Map M2 • 416 977 2320 • www. neill-wycik.com • $*

5 Victoria's Mansion Inn and Guest House

In the heart of Toronto's Gay and Lesbian Village on a tree-lined street, this charming small hotel, with a lovely Victorian-style garden, provides a respite from the bustle of the city. All rooms come with private baths, and suites are equipped with amenities such as a fridge and microwave. Free parking. ✆ *68 Gloucester St • Map L1 • 416 921 4625 • www. victoriasmansion.com • $$*

6 Castlegate Inn

Close to Casa Loma, three Victorian houses have been linked together to make a small hotel offering rooms and apartments at affordable rates. All come with a private bath, mini-fridge, and microwave. ✆ *219 Spadina Rd • Map C2 • 416 323 1657 • www.castle gateinn.com • $*

7 The Grange Hotel and Apartments

Each studio room in this six-floor hotel is equipped with a kitchenette and bath. Stays are for a minimum of three nights. ✆ *165 Grange Ave • Map H3 • 416 603 7700 • www. grangehotel.com • $*

8 Global Village Backpackers

Just south of Chinatown, this hostel has its own lively in-house bar and an outdoor patio. Beds are in dorms, rooms for four, or a few private rooms. Bathrooms are shared. ✆ *460 King St W • Map H4 • 416 703 8540 • www. globalbackpackers.com • $*

9 Hostelling International Toronto

Offering mainly shared rooms in dorms, although there are a few private rooms with private bath, a stay here is one of the cheapest in the city. It is located just south of the Gay Village. ✆ *76 Church St • Map L4 • 416 971 4440 • www.hostelling toronto.com • $*

10 Hostelling International Niagara Falls

A short walk from the falls, this hostel is especially well kept. No private baths, but some private rooms, along with dorms and four-bed rooms. ✆ *4549 Cataract Ave, Niagara Falls • Map Q3 • 905 357 0770 • www. hostellingniagara.com • $*

General Index

Index

Acknowledgments

The Authors
Lorraine Johnson is the author of several books and coauthor of Dorling Kindersley's Eyewitness guide to Chicago. She also writes regularly for magazines on gardening and environmental issues. She lives in Toronto.

Barbara Hopkinson is a writer and editor who has directed a wide range of international publishing projects. She lives in Toronto.

Produced by International Book Productions Inc., Toronto

Editorial Director
Barbara Hopkinson
Art Editor James David Ellis
Senior Editor Judy Phillips
Senior DTP Designer
Dietmar Kokemohr
Photo Research and Permissions
Sheila Hall
Proofreader Ken Ramstead
Indexer Barbara Sale Schon
Photographer Cylla von Tiedemann

SPECIAL THANKS: Raj Rama, Ontario Tourism Marketing Partnership; Lou Seiler, Casa Loma; Michael Snow; Renée Tratch, Royal Ontario Museum

AT DORLING KINDERSLEY
Senior Art Editor Marisa Renzullo
Senior Editor Kathryn Lane
Publishing Manager Kate Poole
Publisher Douglas Amrine
Senior Cartographic Editor
Casper Morris
Senior DTP Designer Jason Little
Production Rita Sinha
Maps Simonetta Giori, Dominic Beddow (Draughtsman Ltd)
Picture Researchers Rhiannon Furbear, Ellen Root, Romaine Werblow
Editorial & Design Assistance
Mark Bailey, Lydia Baillie, Sonal Bhatt, Ilona Biro, Mariana Evmolpidou, Maite Lantaron, Marianne Petrou, Mani Ramaswamy, Quadrum Solutions.

Picture Credits
t-top; tl-top left; tlc-top left centre; tc-top centre; tr-top right; cla-centre left above; ca-centre above; cra-centre right above; cl-centre left; c-centre; cr-centre right; clb-centre left below; cb-centre below; crb-centre right below; bl-bottom left, b-bottom; bc-bottom centre; bcl-bottom centre left; br-bottom right; d-detail.

Every effort has been made to trace the copyright holders, and we apologize for any unintentional omissions. We would be pleased to insert the appropriate acknowledgments in any subsequent edition of this publication.

The publishers would like to thank the following individuals, companies, and picture libraries for their kind permission to reproduce their photographs:

ART GALLERY OF ONTARIO: Albrecht Dürer, German 1471–1528, *Adam and Eve*, 1504, engraving on laid paper 24.7 x 19.1 cm 17bc; Claude Monet, French 1840–1926, *Vétheuil en été*, 1879, oil on canvas 67.7 x 90.5 cm 17tl; The work illustrated on page 16bc is reproduced by permission of the Henry Moore Foundation; Claes Oldenburg, American b.1929, *Floor Burger*, 1962, canvas filled with foam rubber and cardboard boxes painted with acrylic paint 132.1 x 213.4 cm, purchased 1967 72cra; Michael Snow, Canadian b.1929, *Venus Simultaneous*, 1962, oil on canvas and wood 299.7 x 200.7 cm 6bl, 17cra; Tom Thomson, Canadian 1877–1917, *The West Wind*, 1917, oil on canvas 120.7 x 137.9 cm, Gift of the Canadian Club of Toronto, 1926 16–17c

BATA SHOE MUSEUM: Hal Roth 74c
BUDDIES IN BAD TIMES THEATRE: 50c